Southern Gothic

Joe Tallarigo

Southern Gothic

Copyright © 2020 Twin Hills Publishing LLC

All rights reserved. No part of this book may be used or reproduced by any means, graphic, electronic, or mechanical, including photocopying, recording, taping, or by any information storage retrieval without the written consent of the publisher except brief quotations embodied in critical articles and reviews.

Written by and interior designed by Joe Tallarigo

Front and back cover designed by Alaina Broughton

Published by Twin Hills Publishing LLC

ISBN: 978-1-7329930-2-0

This is a work of fiction. All characters, names, incidents, organizations, and dialogue in this book are the product of the author's imagination or are used fictitiously.

Unless noted by the author.

A word from the Author

I was three years old when I had my first encounter with the paranormal and had many more encounters in my young life. I also enjoy watching shows about paranormal activities and finding new places supposedly haunted.

When presented with tales and stories I have a dose of skepticism and look for natural answers, but sometimes there are no answers. I believe that everyone has their own beliefs and skepticism and what we believe is our own opinion.

This book goes out to all those who believe in the paranormal.
This book goes out for those who are on the fence about their beliefs in the paranormal.
This book goes out for the skeptics who don't believe in the paranormal even with proof.

Fun trivia:
Apartment #9 is the ninth poem.
Friday the Thirteenth is the thirteenth poem.
Woke up and was Twenty-One is the twenty-first poem.
Ghost of Christmas present is the twenty-fifth poem.
Halloween Blues is the thirty-first poem.

Chapter One

Southern Gothic Rising

The worldwide community of the Paranormal

Bright lights, UFOS, aliens, abductions, getting probed
dense forests, skunk odor, broken branches
big footprints in the snow
is the Loch Ness monster a prehistoric dinosaur
does the Mothman still appear before tragedies
that's one part of the paranormal

Demons, evil spirits, getting scratched and possessed
portals to hell
talking and walking dolls
with toys turning on with no batteries
hearing loud footsteps on the second floor
when you're home alone
and hearing conversations in your room as you're sleeping
that's another part of the paranormal

Esp, astrology, tarot cards, crystal balls
palm readers, mediums, Ouija boards, fortune tellers
we all want to know our future
and talk to our loved ones who passed on
that's the third part of the paranormal

Hallway stairs, dark closets, damp basements,
and cobwebbed attics
night terrors, glowing red eyes staring at you
evil clowns, muscle man, roaring lions, the ringmaster
ride the midnight circus train of horror, that's the last part of
the paranormal

Put them all together to form
the worldwide community of the paranormal
things that mystified and scared us for thousands of years
some go on the hunt to prove that it exists
some cower in fear under their blankets
while others deny it's even real with proof
what you believe is up to you.

I want to Believe

I want to believe
there's more to this life
that we can't explain with our carnal mind
that there's a spiritual world
connected to our world
that our souls keep existing
long after we're dead

I want to believe
there are other planets like ours
light-years away that we can't see
that aliens visited the earth thousands of years ago
to help our ancestors build the pyramids
and other ancient structures
that they gave them the technology
and wisdom to understand the universe

I want to believe
bigfoot and other monsters
live hidden in their habitats
staying far away from humans
to coexist in peace
only to appear from time to time
to give us a mystery
that there's more to Earth
than meets the eye

I want to believe
there's a spiritual battle
between good and evil
because the world is getting turned upside down
truths are becoming lies, and lies are becoming truths
there's a lot at stake
as both sides dig in deep in their beliefs
while the middle ground erodes away

I want to believe
we connect to certain people
angels that help us on our journey
guide us through our uncertainties
to light a path we can't see
to help us understand our ways
may not always be the right way

No! I need to believe these things
for if not, then I can't explain
all that I've experienced
from seeing ghosts, having nightmares since I was three
that I survived the pain and misery
thanks to God with His love and mercy
I believe in Him
though I struggle with my faith
by believing in the paranormal.

Southern Gothic Rising

Southern horror in the moonlight
southern legends that'll give you a fright
southern monsters emerge from the deep
southern ghosts will haunt your dreams

Ivy climbs up the wall of manors
preachers preach on the slyness of the devil
if you're not careful and let your guard down
both can strangle and lay you in the ground

Gargoyles guard cathedrals
gnomes watch over gardens
scarecrows protect the crops
dogs defend our houses

Southern Gothic all around us
black clouds sneak up on the sun
fire burns in our children's eyes
as evil spirits roam the night

Ravens sit outside windows
crocodiles take over swamps
owls hunt in the woods
opossums take shelter in garbage cans

Lonesome roads, dense forests
churches with cemeteries
civil war battlefields
all have secrets to discover

Southern Gothic is a lifestyle
only a few can handle
a fine line between good and evil
do you believe in the paranormal
or dare to discover the truths about the spiritual world
and see how brave you are

Southern Gothic rising in the night
get ready for a long and twisted ride.

Alabama Nights

Whiskey in a jug
sitting on a cob-webbed porch
the Montgomery stars are shining bright
mosquitoes and gnats swarm in the air
a southern breeze brings in the humidity
the scarecrow in the garden is thirsty
he wants a swig of that whiskey
there's nothing weird here
it's just an ordinary Alabama night

Teens drive the back roads
searching for evidence to local legends
of ghosts, monsters, and hauntings
when they come upon cry baby bridge in Saraland
they heard a woman threw her baby off the bridge
then she jumped in and both drowned
and you can still hear their mournful cries
they pull out their digital voice recorders
hoping to catch some EVP's
on this ordinary Alabama night

A young girl stares into her mirror
as she brushes her long blond hair
preparing for bed
unaware of a black mass
is forming above her head
she will have a nightmare
when she closes her eyes
they will hear her screams throughout Birmingham
on this ordinary Alabama night

Southern Gothic

The scarecrow now sits on the cob-webbed porch
drinking the whiskey from the jug
the Montgomery stars are shining bright
mosquitoes and gnats swarm in the air
a southern breeze brings in the humidity
there's nothing weird here
it's just an ordinary Alabama night.

Driving Lost

It's much too dark, a little too quiet
it's not what I like
as I drive lost on these deserted country roads
searching for my grandparent's house
that they recently moved into
my headlights, my only guide
as I enter a twilight mist
I have an unpleasant feeling
I will not survive this drive

I come upon a church
lit up by floodlights
an evil spirit or demon wouldn't dare come near
but say a prayer just in case
I turn on the radio for company
but I only get static
this drive isn't what I expected
when I told them I would drop by

The mist grows into a thick blanket
it's getting harder to see what's in front of me
two glowing lights appear in my line of sight
I step on the brakes and come to a sudden stop
only to discover it's a doe blocking the road
as if an omen I should go back home
I honk my horn
the doe scurries into the woods
and I travel on

I come upon a graveyard
two buzzards sit on top of the iron gate
I make a sign of the cross for those buried there
a slight gesture to make sure no spirits follow me
I make it a half-mile when I hear a girl speak
from my back seat
she says, "I too was on my way to my grandparents' house
when all the roads became twisted
I ended up all over the place
I couldn't find my way home and finally went mad
I jumped into the lake that's up ahead,"

I blink a few times, but she's still there
her brown hair and clothes now soaked
she continues, "I'm here to help you survive
you must turn around before you reach the bridge
or you'll go mad, and jump into the lake
an icy shiver runs up my spine
I know she isn't lying
so I make a quick U-turn

I drive back the way I came
the girl disappears as I pass her grave
I come upon the church
the bells toll
as something hits me hard in the gut
I stop the car in terror as it comes back to me
my grandparents died seven years ago
so why am I driving on these back roads?

Southern Gothic Girl

Southern gothic girl, bring me into your world
take your time with me
there's no rush
I want to sit around a table with lit candles
holding hands with your friends
as we conjure up the secrets of the past
while being visited by the dead

In your eyes I see portals
connected to worlds I can't explain
black shadows follow you all over town
will you give me a tour of New Orleans
the one that exists after sundown
when the spirits are free to roam
I want to feel right at home

Take me to the bayous
with the crocodiles, moss, and muddy waters
as the harvest moon rises
let's search the land for buried treasure
left behind by the pirates from the 1800s

Southern gothic girl, I hope to meet
the ghost of Marie Laveau, the voodoo queen
as she wanders through Saint Louis cemetery
so she can create a spell for me
that will help you see
I want you to be my Morticia to my Gomez
because I love you, southern gothic girl.

The Beast

What's seven feet tall
covered from head to toe in thick fur
has glowing red eyes, makes me want to cry out in fright
I'm not sure, but it's standing right behind you
I can feel his furious breath from here
his fanged teeth ready to bite down
his enormous claws ready to swipe
are you also frozen in fear as I am

His skunk odor crinkles up my nose
I now see the terror in your eyes
wondering if I'm coming up with a plan
that will get us out of here
or at least give us a fighting chance
since he has the home-field advantage

I gaze upon a branch and pick it up
I give you the nod as I aim it at the beast
as you bolt towards me
the beast gives chase
I launch the branch to slow him down
he howls, then growls as it hits him
we run towards the clearing
knowing time and distance is not on our side
branches and twigs break behind us
as he lunges at us in stride
I never imagined our hike would turn out like this

What's seven feet tall
covered from head to toe in thick fur
has glowing red eyes, makes me want to cry out in fright
I don't know, but there's several around us closing in
our last breaths are here
it looks like we're their bedtime snack
since there's nowhere to run or hide.

Chapter Two

Haunted places and Trains

Dormant

Ordinary looking houses can be deceitful
though they look calm and peaceful
the land they sit on
can harbor residue from the past
people from hundreds of years ago
could have conjured up demons
and other evil spirits

Dormant they stay
waiting patiently to enter the house
feeding off fear, anger, and resentment
growing more powerful
unleashing unholy terror
on those who are weak or scared
by scratching and growling at them
causing nightmares
and appear as black shadows or hellish creatures
they won't stop until they tear apart the happy family

They stir from their slumber
when renovations on the house occur
they don't want the new owners to change a thing
they want the house to remain as it is
or they protect a dark secret they kept hidden in life
so it's never revealed in the light

Dormant they stay
waiting patiently to enter the house
feeding off fear, anger, and resentment
growing more powerful
unleashing unholy terror
on those who are weak or scared
by scratching and growling at them
causing nightmares
and appear as black shadows or hellish creatures
they won't stop until they tear apart the happy family.

Joe Tallarigo

Apartment #9

I drift off to sleep after a hard day's work
of moving my furniture and possessions
into my new apartment
when someone stomps around above me
great, I have a noisy neighbor
it's a quarter to midnight
and I must get up at six A.M.

I pull my pillows over my ears
to drown out the noise
but I jump in fear
as a loud crash shakes my room
I curse under my breath
pound on the ceiling
hoping they stop making so much noise

I get back under my covers
but peace doesn't come
as my bedroom door slowly creaks open
then quickly slams shut
I turn on my table lamp
stare in shock
as the door continues to open and slam on its own

Must be a draft, I think to myself
no need to get scared
as I ease back into sleep, a tv blares
Bam! Bam! Bam!
someone is banging on my front door
I get out of bed
to see who it is

"Can you keep it down, my son is trying to sleep,"
a woman in curlers says to me
before I can reply
all the cabinet doors open and shut
she screams out in fear
as she races down the hall and stairs
leaving me alone, now frightened

I must discover what's going on
I walk up the stairs to the third floor
as I knock loudly on apartment nines door
a thick dark feeling comes over me
"open up we need to talk,"
the apartment door behind me opens
a man walks out and says no one lives there

My face gets flush my heart skips a beat
he says "you must be new here
the original tenant of apartment nine
had a feud with the tenant of apartment five
one night they came to blows, and he died
he swore he would take his revenge
on anyone who rents apartment five,"

I shake off the story I'm not scared anymore
he can't make me move out by making noises
I go back to my apartment
the stomping continues
I ignore his commotions
I peacefully drift off to sleep
hoping he'll tire out and will stop haunting me.

Haunted Bar

Welcome to my haunted bar
don't be afraid that the barkeep is a skeleton
and the waitress is a vampire
don't worry she won't bite
don't jump in fright if you get touched from behind
and you don't see anyone
it's only the ghosts saying hi
we're all here for an eerie time

The banshees are taking the stage
spiders emerge from their corners to get a good seat
would you mind having the first dance
with the bride who perished on her wedding day
it's Friday the thirteenth with a full moon
take a howl with the werewolves at midnight
you're in the right place
if you're looking for a night of fright

The zombies are bringing their best ghouls
to dance with all night long
come have a drink with Doctor Frankenstein
he'll talk your ear off about his latest creations
but don't look alive or into his eyes
he may discover you're a perfect match
and use you in one of his monsters

The devil himself appeared here in 1979
claimed he could turn the water into wine
he then challenged a priest to a game of darts
said we'll play for all your parishioner's souls
but if you win, I'll go back to hell
the devil threw all bullseye's
as did the priest
in sudden death as the devil got ready to throw
he got distracted by a vixen in a bright red dress
and missed the board
the priest threw another bullseye for the win
the devil got upset and unleashed his minions
the priest put up a good fight
he locked all the demons away
at the bottom of the whiskey bottle
then banished the devil back to hell.

Summer Wind

I wish Summer Wind mansion was still standing
so we can have an understanding
of what occurred there
what's fact and what's fiction
was there a curse upon the land
did ghosts roam the halls
or was it something more sinister
that tormented the owners of the mansion
causing everyone to flee in panic and fear
or was it all legend

Who did Mr. Lamont fire his gun at
in front of the basement door
with the bullets passing through the apparition
and ended up lodged in the door
did that cause them to flee that same night
and never return

Summer Wind, what's your secret
that you've kept hidden all these years
was there a curse upon the land
did ghosts roam your halls
or was it something more sinister
that tormented the owners of the mansion
causing them all to flee in panic and fear

Why were the workers and contractors scared
to go into the mansion and help the Hinshaw's
renovate and remodel the rooms
who or what possessed Arnold
causing him to play demonic music on the organ
all night long

Summer Wind, will we ever discover the truth
of who or what roamed your halls
or will you keep your secret hidden forever
no matter how many people search for clues
it may always remain a mystery
since something scares everyone away
and we can't investigate your mansion
because in 1988 you burnt to the ground
after lightning struck you
leaving only two chimneys behind.

Ghost Train 369

My grandpa called me into the living room
said let me tell you a story before you go to bed
he threw a log onto the fire, and in a haunting voice he said

It was a warm spring night in 1959
I was twenty-four heading home to my new bride
I was in a private compartment on train #369
reading the newspaper to pass the time
when the door handle turned
followed by four knocks, with a man saying
can I join you, I could use the company

I put down my paper, opened the door
to see a pale man standing there looking scared
concerned, I said come on in would you like a drink
he said give me some whiskey, and I'll be fine
I've been traveling for too long
and hope tonight is my last ride

In the bright light, I saw something was off
his eyes were pale and wore a torn shirt
with dusty overalls, his hair and beard were rugged
as if he just stepped out of the dust bowl
he said to me
believe what I'm about to tell you
I'm a prisoner on this train
only you can set me free

The room grew cold as a chill ran up my spine
I nervously laughed, didn't know what to say
he saw I didn't believe him, so he continued
let me guess you recently got married
but your job took you away
before you could go on your honeymoon
now you're hurrying home to your bride to make things right

How did you know, I replied in shock
just then the train went dark, and he began to glow
he said you're on a ghost train
tonight is the anniversary of the crash
I was on this train in 1932 to meet up with my bride
when a storm blew out of nowhere
the engineer and crew did all they could
but the train jumped the tracks, and everyone perished

I was cursed to ride this train
until I met another man who postponed his honeymoon
you must jump off before the storm blows in
and when you do, I'll finally be free
just then there was a roar of thunder
rain fell on the windows
we need to hurry he said
as he guided me to an exit door
I jumped off, and the train disappeared

"Oh, grandpa, ghost trains are just legends," I said
he reached behind his chair
producing a framed ticket of train #369
dated September 13, 1959
along with a newspaper with the headlines about the crash
dated September 13, 1932.

Chapter 3

Terror in the Night

Friday the Thirteenth

The alarm clock didn't go off, and the coffee didn't brew
your son is crying, has a fever of one hundred and two
he can't go to preschool
so you call your mom to babysit
you check your bank account while waiting for her to arrive
only to discover your paycheck wasn't deposited
you throw your arms in the air
wondering what else could go wrong

After your mom arrives, you walk out to your car
only to discover the back tire is flat
as you call for a cab
a black cat runs across your path
the blue sky is turning dark
rain begins to fall
you're ready to give up

It's Friday the thirteenth
a superstitious day you never believed in
but the coincidences are piling up quick
you think about calling in sick
but decide to push on as the cab arrives

You arrive at work an hour late
the elven A.M. meeting has started two hours early
you apologize to your boss as you open your briefcase
only to discover it's empty
you turn red, feel flush
explain how your son was sick
and rushed out of the house

It's Friday the thirteenth
you should have gone back to bed
instead of trying to push on
and make gold out of hay
we all have our bad days
just push it out of your mind
but when the next Friday the thirteenth come around
maybe take the day off and stay home.

When the night Comes

As the sun sets behind the mountains
pine trees come alive supplying a cold breeze
stars dot the velvet sky
wolves, bats, opossums, stir
to make their evening rounds
it's time to find a secure place
block all the doors and cover all the windows
turn on all the lights
to keep the evil at bay

When the night comes, it beckons evil, takes over
restless spirits rise from their graves
to take revenge on the living
no one is safe
when they're outside
so take heed when you see the signs
that darkness is falling across the land
so you can protect yourself
from the evil

Another sleepless night comes
as you take shelter in your farmhouse
hoping that the batteries in your flashlight
can last all night
and the ragged quilts you have
will secure all the windows and doors
as the sun sets there are sounds of branches breaking
is it an animal or spirits coming to take their revenge
even though you're innocent

When the night comes, it beckons evil, takes over
restless spirits rise from their graves
to take revenge on the living
no one is safe
when they're outside
so take heed when you see the signs
that darkness is falling across the land
so you can protect yourself
from the evil.

The old country Winds

The old country winds are howling tonight
making the shutters slam against the windows
dead leaves dance in the fields
tree limbs creak as they sway
a cold draft seep into my room
I tightly pull my comforter over my head
I have an irrational fear of the old country winds
that howl in the night

It began when I was seven
trying to get comfortable in my new room
we just my moved to the country
I couldn't get to sleep
without the city traffic and noisy neighbors
when out of the nowhere the wind began howling
the house came alive
dark shadows formed on my wall
from the illumination of the moon

Heavy footsteps stomped in the attic above me
tree limbs scratched against my window
the howling wind sounded like mournful cries
I hid under my covers, hoping my mom and dad realized
that I was scared to death
soon it got so cold I could see my breath
I heard my closet door open
I was shaking in fear
as I felt two hands grab my comforter

My comforter violently lifted off me
An old lady stared at me
her hallowed eyes, disfigured face burnt into my soul
her mouth opened letting out a shriek
I felt her evil encase me
a demon from hell
to give me a warning
that I would never have another peaceful sleep
as long as the old country winds howl

The next morning I hoped it was all a dream
an overactive imagination from being in a new place
but week after week
the old country winds howled
with the elderly demonic lady appearing
shrieking at me so I couldn't sleep
my parents didn't believe me
and said I had an overactive imagination

The old country winds are howling tonight
making the shutters slam against the windows
dead leaves dance in the fields
tree limbs creak as they sway
a cold draft seep into my room
I know the demonic old lady
will soon appear to shriek at me
so I'll have another sleepless night.

Starry Sky

It's a beautiful summer night
staring up at the evening sky
out in the country with no light pollution
getting to see the Milky Way
and the constellations so clearly
millions of stars shine just for you
fireflies your only company
or so you think

A bright light appears in the southern part of the sky
it seems to hover above the tree line
you pay it no attention
it's only an airplane moving slow
so you go back viewing the stars
then out of nowhere, your car radio goes haywire
the car lights turn on by themselves
you realize you're not alone

The bright light is now hovering above you
you see there are no wings
it's a triangular-shaped craft
your heart races as you run
but a bright beam of light blinds you
you're flying into the air
when you open your eyes, you find yourself
surrounded by four-foot grey aliens

They tie you down to a steel table
you hear the rustling of different tools
you know this can't be good
you squirm in the stirrups
pleading to them to let you go
but they probe you all over
and perform experiments

What an unpleasant night this is
traveling through the starry sky
out in the universe
never getting to see the Milky Way
or the constellations ever again
now that you're a prisoner to four-foot aliens
and kept in a metal cage.

Home Alone

The grandfather clock chimes nine times
the oven timer beeps
I search for the pizza cutter, but it's missing
creak, creak, creak, goes the hallway steps
Max, my cat hisses
"quiet," I say
trying to calm my nerves

I pull the pizza from the oven
"mmm," I'm ready to dig in
I grab a plate from the cabinet
whoosh, whoosh, whoosh, frigid air encases me
goosebumps form all over my body
I dare not turn around
for fear I will not like what I see

I jump as someone tugs hard on my shirt
whispers something inaudible in my ear
my plate drops to the floor
thump, thump, thump, loud footsteps are behind me
come on Max, we need to get out of here
I pick him up, run up the hallway stairs
and hide in the bathroom

In the mirror, I see a black shadow appear behind me
I mumble "I'm not afraid, I'm brave, I believe in God
you have no power over me,"
scratch, scratch, scratch, claws dig deep into my skin
my back is burning
I turn around and see
three deep scratches running down my back

Joe Tallarigo

I try to open the door
but it won't open
"Open up," I scream in panic
ha, ha, ha, The black shadow laughs evilly
"I've been watching you for some time
I never liked kids and never will
sorry that your parents will never see you again,"

The black shadow overpowers me
I fall to my knees
knowing I'm about to die
gasp, gasp, gasp, I'm suffocating
a bright light appears before me
"enter the light," a deep growling voice says
as someone shoves me into it

Thump! I awaken on my couch
no one is around
just the glow from the tv screen
"I'm alive," I scream in joy
woo-hoo, woo-hoo, woo-hoo, I sigh
I must have fallen asleep
and had a bad dream
no more scary movies for me

Chime, Chime, Chime,
goes the grandfather clock nine times
buzz, buzz, buzz, goes the oven timer
creak, creak, creak, goes the hallway stairs
hiss, hiss, hiss, goes my cat, Max.

On this dreary Night

I'm wide awake drowning in my depressing thoughts
apparitions appear on my walls
disembodied voices call out my name
but stay quiet when I reply
3 a.m. church bells toll for the dead
honestly, I'm not at peace

On this dreary night, a raven appeared at my window
mocks me for all my sorrows
as snow falls gently to the ground
the wind moans my ex's name
maybe tomorrow she'll see the error in her ways
and will come knocking at my door
she'll love me once more
Oh Loraine, will you love me once again
like you did before

I hold her picture in my hands
it still tears me apart when she said to me
I need to find myself, chase my dreams
but why did she have to leave so quickly
leaving me no chance at having closure
oh Loraine, will you ever come back
whoosh! My front door flies open
"Loraine is that you, Loraine, please answer,"
but there's no reply, only a cold presence
I feel soft lips kiss my cheek
and smell her familiar scent of Vanilla
before I can react
the wind blows the window open
letting the cold and snow in

I close the window, turn off the light, and sigh
try to salvage any sleep I can get
that kiss makes me feel everything will turn out all right
as I drift off to sleep, my phone rings
I quickly answer, "Loraine, is that you?"
"no sir," I'm Officer Robb, a male voice says
"There's been an accident on Route Five
when I arrived, a woman was pleading with me
that I needed to call you and tell you
she was sorry for running off
she was on her way to you to make amends,"
tears form in my eyes
my heart jumps into my throat
knowing what he was going to tell me next

On this dreary night
the ghost of my Loraine visited me
whom I loved since I was sixteen
she came back to me one last time
before she headed into the light.

Nightly Stroll

In the twilight mist, we meet up
hand in hand we stroll through the park
fireflies gather around to guide us
on the deserted paths
I stop along the way to pick wildflowers
and give them to you
I must say you still look like the blushing bride
I married on our wedding day
as we come to the top of the hill
our breath is taken away by the sight
of the moonlight illuminating the river

We sit on a concrete bench
you brush her hand against my cheek
says "I admit I've been weak
without your companionship these past five years
but tonight I'm delighted to be back with you,"
the crickets perform a song
we get up and dance
owls, opossums, raccoons, and rabbits
gather around us as we rekindle our love

As the moonlight fades, giving way to the morning sun
it's time we head back home
hand in hand, we pass through the iron gate
I wrap my arms around you
kiss you on the lips
and say, "I'll see you tonight, my love
same time, same place
on top of our graves."

Girl of the Full Moon

She twirls around in the moonlight
not having a care in the world
out in the woods all alone
she has no fear
her heart tells her she belongs here
her glowing eyes says it all

She's a girl of the full moon
staying out until sunrise
always smiling, feeling alive
as the starlight dances on her skin
everybody tries to reign her in
she assures them she'll be back soon
she's a girl of the full moon

It all began when she was seven
as she watched a full moon rose to heaven
she became friends with the planets and stars
climbed a tree
reached out far as she could
to grab a new piece of her new world

She's a girl of the full moon
staying out until sunrise
always smiling, feeling alive
as the starlight dances on her skin
everybody tries to reign her in
she assures them she'll be back soon
she's a girl of the full moon.

Woke up and I was Twenty-one

Hello God, can you calm my anxious mind
tomorrow is the first day of my senior year
I could use some clarity and guidance
of where I should go to college
or if I should jump right into the workforce
if you could give me advice or a sign
I'd appreciate it, thanks for listening
then I drift off to sleep

The wailing of police sirens awakens me
I'm in a downtown alley
standing over a man with a bullet hole in his chest
I'm holding a gun that may have killed him
I have no recollection of how I got here
or why I was even in the alley
I don't recognize the man
or why I would have shot him

My life is about to change
as the police officers pull up
orders me to drop my gun
an officer puts me in handcuffs
I face a judge and jury
it was a slam dunk case
the judge sentenced me to life in prison
I'm upset and more confused
when they said I was twenty-one years old
how did three years pass by so quickly

A few months later the devil appeared in my cell
said, "do you remember the night you were eighteen
I came to you as an angel of light
convinced you that everyone was leaving you
and your future was bleak
I even fast-forwarded your life by three years
to prove to you what I was saying was true
you ended up homeless and desperate,"

I stared at him with anger
he said, "I'll give you a chance to make things right,"
he snapped his fingers I was back in the alley
the man I killed was standing in front of me
pleading with me not to shoot him
I said, "sir, you'll be okay,"
as I lowered the gun
it went off striking him in the chest
I heard the police sirens screaming towards me
as I was being arrested and hauled away
I stared at the man I shot, and he gave me a wink

I'm still in prison
all because the devil set me up
to shoot him in the chest
when I was twenty-one years old.

See you in the Morning

Let daddy sleep I had a rough day
go back to bed sweetie, snuggle with your teddy bear
there's nothing to be afraid of
I read your favorite stories, kissed you goodnight
I promise everything will be all right
and I'll see you in the morning

I sigh, as I hear her footsteps go back down the hall
I knew this would be rough on her
she didn't understand why she had to leave
I told her it was for the best
she wouldn't be in pain anymore
her illness would go away
she would receive her angel wings
as she reunites with her mom and grandparents

Tears flowed down my face
as I placed her favorite teddy bear in her arms
and laid my eyes on my little girl for the last time
I told her I would be okay
I'd be visiting her grave every morning and night
reading her favorite stories, making up my own
about a strong little girl who fought as long as she could

I also told her she could visit her room
that all her toys, art supplies, and clothes
would always be here for her
so she would forever feel welcome
but I didn't think she would visit so soon
since it was only at noon today
I laid flowers on her grave after her funeral.

Angel of Death

Without warning, he appears in a darkened hall of a hospital
at 3 A.M.
he observes the nurses and doctors around their desks
believing everything is running smoothly
that's when he makes his rounds
searching for the names on his list
when he finds them, he makes them go code blue
he holds their hands as they take their last breath
then guides them into the afterlife

He's the angel of death
misunderstood, feared, and hated
people believe they have all the time in the world
but it's a misconception and lie
they yell and curse at him
why can't he take someone else
but it's not his choice since he's only following orders

Under the night sky, through the fog and rain
he moves like the wind to another head-on crash
he spots the spirits of his victims
hovering over their lifeless bodies
they're confused and upset
as the EMT's ignore their pleas
to rush them to the hospital
they don't understand they're already dead
he makes his way over to them to help them cross over

He's the angel of death
misunderstood, feared, and hated
people believe they have all the time in the world
but it's a misconception and lie
they yell and curse at him
why can't he take someone else
but it's not his choice since he's only following orders

He tries his best to make people feel at ease
when they've been fighting a lengthy battle
as their time on earth is drawing nigh
but they're holding on and not ready to pass on
he brings along their family members who already passed on
to assure their loved one that it's okay to let go
there's a whole new world to explore
where there's no sadness or illness
once they take their final breath

One day or night at your appointed time
you'll meet him
the angel of death.

Christmas Town

I have a shopping list in my pocket
mom says I must be back by three
so we can make all the desserts and side dishes
for tomorrows celebration at the town center
and we need to decorate our Christmas tree
for our family party on Christmas Eve

I walk past the school, church, and bingo hall
a boy and girl stand next to a snowman
I say hi but get no reply
they must be busy in thought
I walk on past and see Santa holding a teddy bear
"Can I have one for my sister," I ask him
but he stands frozen in time just like the boy and girl

My head starts to spin, trying to figure out what's going on
I come upon a taxi stopped in the middle of the street
knowing I can make it to the shops faster
as I pull on the front door handle, it doesn't budge
I knock on the driver's window, but no one answers
"Guess they don't want the fare," I say and walk on

I finally come upon the stores
there's a crowd of people
but they're all staying in place
I'm now freaking out because no one seems to be alive
I pull on the door to the toy store
but it won't open
I look in the window and see a cashier checking out a man
I knock on the window to get their attention
but they don't move

Suddenly, I hear Silver bells blaring on a radio
hear loud footsteps coming towards me
I don't know where the sounds are coming from
I feel a hand grab me around the waist
who moved you in front of the toy store
a woman's voice says
she places me back in front of my house
and walks away

I can't move, my eyes stare at the town in front of me
I wish I could finish Christmas shopping for my mom
but I don't understand why I can't move any more
I live in one weird town.

Ghost of Christmas Present

The bright lights on the Christmas tree
are growing dim
the warmth of the fire is quickly fading
as a frigid airmass takes its place
the presents wrap with love
are being ripped open by unseen hands
the radio is going haywire
with the carols being taken over by shrieks and screams
the smell of sulfur
replaces the aroma of sugar cookies baking in the oven

I'm sitting on my couch bundled up under my blankets
wondering what the hell is going on
am I in the middle of a bad dream
from watching a Christmas Carol all week
or am I being visited by spirits
who want me to change my ways before it's too late
I know I will be up all night
re-wrapping all the presents

The peaceful silence outside is being broken
by howling Canadian winds
sleet and ice pound on the roof and windows
the neighbor's dogs down the way are barking
they want to get in their house
I'm getting scared as the Christmas lights and fire go out
leaving me in total darkness

"Hells Bells!" I exclaim as I get off the couch
I have to find a flashlight and check on my cookies
I stop in fear just as I enter the kitchen
a tall, dark figure with sinister-looking eyes
is standing near the oven
he stares at me
my blood runs cold while my legs turn to stone

He says I had hoped that the chaos in the living room
would have kept you distracted as I snack on these cookies
they are the delicious
but I'm not here to collect your soul
I'm the ghost of Christmas present
just a few minutes early
I'm here for your two cousins
who want to surprise you tonight
but little do they know when they turn on your road
their car will hit an icy patch and spin out of control

"No!" I cry out pulling out my cellphone
I dial my cousin's number, but the call doesn't go through
the storm must have knocked out the telephone lines
"Please reconsider," I beg the hooded figure
but he disappears
I rush out the front door
I hear a car spinning out of control
"I'm too late," I cry out as I hear the crash
and my cousin's screams
I sit on my couch and cry my eyes out
now that my Christmas joy has gone away.

Chapter Four

The week of Halloween

The Veil

The veil between the living and the dead is at its thinnest
as colored leaves get piled up high
the temperatures drop below forty degrees
the sky is always cloudy and gray
kids are dressing up in their costumes
getting ready to go trick-or-treating
jack-o'-lanterns sitting on porches
light the way for the dead to visit the living

On Halloween
as the sun sets in the west
and the moon rises in the east
the portals of the spirit world are open
spirits enter our plane with ease
to give warnings to those on the wrong path
some have unfinished business
and need to complete their tasks

Other spirits are pure evil
who want to continue to torment the living
they harass and attack their victims until they give in
the devil comes up from hell
to collect the victim's soul
the angels in Heaven weep over another lost soul
in the battle between good and evil

Be on the lookout on Halloween
you might see a spirit roaming the Earth.

Ghosts Revenge

Your face burns in my memory
I know what you did
you won't be able to hide from me
I will track you down
so justice can prevail
you're a fugitive on the run
you shot a man in the park
spilling his innocent blood on the ground
ignoring his pleas to call for an ambulance
as you rifled through his wallet

I'm following a few leads
people saw you at two different stores
using his credit cards
don't think you can rest easy and you're in the clear
it might be tomorrow or a week
but I promise I won't give up chasing you
until I track you down

You see, I'm the one you robbed and killed
I stayed in limbo to hunt you down
since I was the only witness
I'm the only one who can bring you to justice
But I wish you would go to the police station on your own
and confess your crimes
so I can cross into the light and be at peace

When I find you and your judgment day comes
if you don't show remorse
I will whisper my name, bang on your walls
move things around, haunt your dreams
until you can't take any more
they'll find your body with your face frozen in fear
it's all up to you how this plays out
I have all of eternity to wait to see justice will prevail.

The abandoned House

It's a dark and dreary night
lightning streaks across the sky
the aroma of rain fills the air
colored leaves rustle in the wind
a car stalls on the one-lane country road
with the woods the only thing around for miles

A young man and woman emerge from the car
both nervous and upset about their situation
they're lost and have no cell-phone reception
they search for help or shelter
but they don't even find a bird or raccoon
then the woman exclaims in glee

She points to a flickering light deep in the woods
she looks at him then he looks at her
"do you think we should check it out?" she asks
he looks up and down the road says, "it can't hurt,"
they make their way through the brush
as tree limbs reach out to grab them

They come upon a three-story house
he steps on the rotted porch
knocks on the front door
"anyone home?" he calls out
but there's only silence
he turns the knob, says "let's go in,"

Vivid lightning provides adequate light as they look around
the young woman pulls the white sheets off the furniture
picks up a golden picture frame off an end table
she gets lightheaded and dizzy
her stomach ties up in knots
she tries to speak, but no words come out

"Darling, what's wrong?" the man asks
she takes a deep breath and says
"does this place look familiar to you?"
he turns from her to study the room
turns white as a ghost
as the firewood in the fireplace bursts into a roaring fire

He says "it's all coming back to me
I remember in my last breath
I promised we would return to our house
for one night every October on the anniversary
when our car skidded off the road
just a few feet from our house
because of the rain and wet leaves
and every year, we have this conversation."

In My Grave

Honey, what's going on
I'm all alone
in a dark and damp place
I only see white velvet
in front of my face
my arms are cross against my chest
why am I wearing my best vest

I can't hear a thing
am I in a dream
honey, try to wake me up
I want to get out of here
I'm scared
come on, shake me awake
don't wait any longer
can't you see I'm struggling to wake up

Mud and dirt fall on me
I can barely breathe
honey, will you bring me a glass of water
to quench my thirst
I can't lift my arms
it seems I've lost all my strength
I need to get up, but can't
can you assist me

What am I feeling on me
something wet and slippery
is slithering up my leg
honey, can you get it off me
now I sense something else
crawling up my neck
eight prickly legs tickle me
I feel the pain of its fangs
piercing my skin

Oh God, am I in the ground
is that my woman can't help me
and the reason I'm all alone
how did I not realize I passed away
but why am I wide awake
is this the afterlife, my eternal paradise
being alive in my grave.

Haunted Hayride II

I'm back for another thirty-one days and nights
of hell and fright
it's my pleasure to be your chauffeur
for your last ride on earth
take a seat on the hay, get comfortable
for a five-mile moonlit ride
passing by barns, cornfields, woods, and graveyard

Hell hounds are patrolling the woods
for anyone who tries to escape
their teeth are sharp like a cold steel blade
that'll puncture your skin
the zombies you see walking around
that's no make-up or costumes
they are genuine, the real walking dead
brought back to life
to give an extra layer of terror
on this haunted hayride

The trees will soon come alive
they'll use their branches to reach out to you
grabbing, clawing, and pinching
at least one is permitted to take a rider
to feast on their skin and bones
the vampires who live amongst the treetops
will also join in to have a drink of their blood

Don't fear or fret most of you will survive
that is until we reach the graveyard
where I already carved your names into your graves
but before we reach your final destination
there are wicked clowns, scarecrows, unworldly beasts
lurking in the cornfields and woods
who have their own twisted ways of scaring you
and causing panic attacks

Are you ready to begin your final journey
on this haunted hayride
it's my pleasure to be your chauffeur
a spirit of the underworld
to take you to your next home
in the afterlife.

Halloween Blues

I have the Halloween blues
I'm too old to go trick-or-treating
but too young to stay out all night
my friends and I don't know what to do
since tomorrow we have school
I wish someone gave me a warning
that being on a teen on Halloween
is a challenging thing to do

I remember when I got scared easily
now there's no more mystery to Halloween
I'm no longer afraid of the scary props
or afraid of the dark
I realized all that fear was in my mind
now I must find something to do
to kill the time
on this Halloween night

I have the Halloween blues
I'm too old to go trick-or-treating
but too young to stay out all night
my friends and I don't know what to do
since tomorrow we have school
I wish someone gave me a warning
that being on a teen on Halloween
is a challenging thing to do

I want to go to a haunted house
where genuine ghosts roam the halls
or to a secluded graveyard
where the restless spirits rise
I'll even go hiking in the woods
where beasts chase down their prey
I need to come face to face
with the paranormal to get over these

Halloween blues
I'm too old to go trick-or-treating
but too young to stay out all night
my friends and I don't know what to do
since tomorrow we have school
I wish someone gave me a warning
that being on a teen on Halloween
is a challenging thing to do.

The scarecrow Walks

He emerges from the cornfields
onto the one-lane country road
he stretches out his arms and legs
thankful to be free
for one week during Halloween
he has permission to be alive
all the kids assume
he's just another trick-or-treater in a costume
making his rounds house to house

He's not going to scare away crows tonight, oh no
he's hunting the kids
who poked and pulled the hay from his chest and arms
thinking they were doing no harm
now it's time for his revenge
one by one he'll drag the kids away
take them to a barn and work his magic

Day after day
new scarecrows pop up in the fields around town
the adults whisper their concerns
they know if they talk too loudly, they'll be next
for they were once kids
and knew the secret of the scarecrow
they all had friends disappear
so they warn their kids to stay out of the cornfields
but kids will be kids

Now the kids hang on their wooden posts
their bodies made of hay
with the faces painted with a wicked smile
day by day their eyes shift around
their only two jobs are to scare away the crows
and take the names of the kids who pull their hay.

The Jack-O'-Lanterns Revenge

She carved his eyes, nose, and mouth
brought him to life by candlelight
he sat proudly on her porch
enjoyed watching the kids and adults
walk by on Halloween night

Ten days after Halloween
she picked him up said
"sorry that I have to do this
but I no longer have any use for you,"
and took him to the garbage can

As she lifted the lid to the garbage can
to throw him in
she suddenly stopped
like magic from a fairy tale
the trees began to sway
a blast of freezing air surrounded her
heavy snow fell
she was put in a trance by the snowflakes
forced to build a snowman
used branches for his arms
coal for his eyes
then a fiendish voice commanded her
to use the jack-o'-lantern for the head

As she placed the jack-o'-lantern
on the snowman's body
her trance broke
she fell in shock and fear
as the snowman came to life

He gave the woman an evil smile
said, "thanks for giving me life,
but I no longer have any use for you,"
he waved his arms causing a flash freeze
she became frozen in place
the next day she melted away
while the snowman made his escape.

Chapter Five

Midnight Horror

Midnight horror Show

She was a new classmate in the nightly acting class
that I was taking
I wanted to impress her by showing I wasn't afraid
of ghosts, monsters, or slasher films
so I asked her to see a midnight horror movie
I figured if she would freak out
she would put her arms around me
but I was wrong
not once did she show any signs of being scared
she even ate her popcorn slowly during the movie

As we were walking home
she said, "come back to my house
I know it's late, but I don't want to be alone
I only put on a brave during the movie
being new in town I'm terrified
please stay with me for a while,"
before I could respond
she grabbed my hand and pulled on my arm
my heart pounded as I realized she was leading me
through the woods of Harrisburg
with the adjoining cemetery

I said, "Kathy, let me give you advice
no one enters these woods at night
even in the daytime, no one visits the cemetery
there has to be another way to your house,"
she replied, "I thought you weren't afraid
of ghosts or monsters
it's the living you should be afraid of,"

Joe Tallarigo

I followed her trying to brave
half-way through the woods
she stopped and turned to me
her face was pale
her eyes had an evil green tint
she bared her teeth, revealing fangs
and says "we're home, and I have to say
you're the best date I had in years
usually, the guys run away before they enter the woods
but you, there's something about you,"
she ran her fingers through my hair, touched my face
"let me make you immortal
so we can be together forever,"

I didn't move or flinch, I just laughed
"nice fake teeth, make-up, and contacts
are you showing off your acting skills
Bravo! You make a convincing vampire,"
suddenly the dark clouds opened up
revealing a full moon, I heard the fluttering of wings
I looked up to see dozens of bats swooping down
she said, "meet my family, we've been here since the 1800s
always on the hunt for fresh blood
and I choose you to be with for all of eternity,"

She grabbed my hand, put me in a trance
bit into my neck
flew me to the treetops
I screamed in pain as four fangs
pushed out my canine teeth
now she and I only come out at night
to take in the midnight horror shows.

Love at first bite

Red dress, red lipstick, hypnotizing eyes
the music draws me close to you
you take me by my hand, tenderly put me at ease
all my worries seep out of my feet
I'm weak as you lean me back as everything does dark

I fell in love at first bite
what a night this turned out to be
a beautiful temptress who chose me
to be your man for eternity
we'll live amongst the treetops
travel the world during the witching hour
the moonlight will be our guide as we fly amongst the stars
I'm in love, love at first bite

I come back around in your arms
the effect of your kiss has taken over
I rush you outside, the dark clouds part
revealing the harvest moon
my heart is pounding as I gaze into your eyes
you giggle knowing this will be a long night

I fell in love at first bite
what a night this turned out to be
a beautiful temptress who chose me
to be your man for eternity
we'll live amongst the treetops
travel the world during the witching hour
the moonlight will be our guide as we fly amongst the stars
I'm in love, love at first bite.

Howling Wolves

Howling wolves on the mountainside
on a moonless night can give anyone a fright
are they howling to let the other wolves in the pack
they are ready to search for a new place
to scour for shelter and rest
or are they hungry and found their next meal
and ready to attack

You might want to turn back
when you wander into their territory
better safe than sorry
especially when the sun has set
and you're all alone in the woods
glowing eyes in the brush will stalk you
until they feel it's the right time to pounce

Ahh-Woo, their howls are getting louder
they're closing in
branches break under their weight
you feel their hot breath surround you
what shall become of you
do you run, do you scream
or stand around

Howling wolves on a mountainside
on a moonless night can frighten anyone.

Run, Run, Run

Karen, you're slowing us down
can't you hear the galloping hoofbeats
stomping hard on the ground
don't you feel the fiery breath
of the stallion that's chasing us
I told you there was a curse in Carrolton woods
but no, I had to listen to you and Bobby
now we need to run, run, run

Watch out for tree roots sticking up from the ground
I don't need anyone getting a twisted ankle
but that's the least of our problems
I can't find the way out
I'm going in circles
we're going to die by fright
or by the fiery eyes that I see staring at us
we need to run, run, run

We come to a sudden stop
a black stallion with a ghostly rider
with fire around his head blocks our escape
he pulls on the reins
the stallion rears
our fear level rises to two hundred percent
we only have a slim chance to survive
we need to run, run, run

Behind us, the galloping hoofbeats keep up with us
as evil laughter emits from the fiery rider
my heart rises to my throat
Karen and Bobby are right beside me
I know if we want to live we can't stick together
I breathy whisper "let's separate
and run, run, run,"

The stallion and fiery rider come to a stop
trying to decide which one of us to chase
I look back, stare into his hollowed-out eyes
I feel his evil resonate in my soul
but to my surprise, he chases Bobby
I hear his chilling screams, then Kara's pleas
oh God, I'm the only one left
he comes upon me I'm too exhausted
to run, run, run

He says, "I haven't had this much fun in over fifty years
most of the kids know to stay out of these woods
they're right no one makes it out alive
but tonight, I'll make an exception
I'm going to make you immortal as a young boy
in exchange, you're going to lure kids into these woods
assuring them, they have nothing to fear
then I'll appear out of the shadows
chase them through the woods
as they run, run, run."

The Creeper

He's in bed watching a black mass
crawl across his ceiling
even in the dark, their eyes lock
fear runs through his veins
as he recognizes the black mass
from the basement of the Wyatt house
the paranormal tour guide warned everyone
there was a creeper who would follow anyone home
who taunted and dared to do its worst

The man saw the black mass in the basement
he taunted and provoked it in his mind
thought he was safe since he said nothing out loud
now his heart pounds, and sweat pours down his body
as the room grows thick and heavy
while the black mass hovers right above him

His skin tingles
as a thousand spiders crawl all over his body
the laughter of clowns fills the room
with a calliope playing
he sees the image of a circus at night
with lions roaring as the trainer holds a chair
trapeze artists go flying in the air
the elephants go on parade
the clowns are throwing pies into each other faces
it's too much for him to take

He screams, "make it stop, make it stop
stop terrorizing me with my darkest fears
why didn't I listen to the tour guide
why did I have to taunt you
I beg you for your mercy
and I promise I'll never taunt the spirits again,"

The black mass fades away
the tingling of his skin, the image of the circus disappears
he feels relieved and drifts peacefully off to sleep
but at three A.M. he wakes up screaming
his deepest darkest fear was coming true
there was no way to stop it
he will live forever facing it

What his deepest darkest fear is I won't say
I'll leave it up to your imagination
as it might be one of your deepest darkest fears.

Secret thoughts of Dolls

You're my best friend
taking me everywhere you go
placing me across from you at your table
pouring me an imaginary cup of tea
I love feeling the wind against my face
as we go down the slide together
you're always gentle as you brush my hair

I don't care if I get mud on my dress
you always take a damp cloth to wipe it off
you make sure I'm sitting upright on the shelf
when you're not home
you hold me tenderly while you sleep
when your friends want to hold me
you make sure their hands are clean

I'm your confidant when you need someone to talk to
I comfort you when you're scared
of the stormy weather
I'm always by your side so you won't feel lonely
I still recall how excited you were when you opened me up
on your sixth birthday

Joe Tallarigo

You're now a teen getting more mature
the things that once brought you joy
are now childish
you're into music, shopping, and boys
little by little you get rid of your things
hoping that another girl will enjoy
your stuffed animals and toys

I'm relieved when you tape another box shut
and take it to the thrift store
while I'm still here on your shelf
knowing I won't be tossed into a bin
and disregarded as junk
with a price tag of $2.99 placed on my bum
for I am worth more than that

Be warned if you choose to get rid of me
I know all your secrets and fears
where you live, where you sleep
I'd hate to unleash my evil upon you
to haunt your dreams
and chase you through your house
I might be a doll to you
but I was made to bring you joy
and I have feelings too.

She needs me So

Why does she need me so
why can't she let me go
why does she appear in my dreams
and haunt my memories

Why are there footprints in the snow
I haven't been outside today
no mail was delivered, it's Sunday
who could have been walking in my yard

There's a scent of her perfume
every time I walk into a room
jasmine and roses
were her favorite choices

Why does she need me so
why can't she let me go
why does she appear in my dreams
and haunt my memories

Why do I hear laughter
coming from down the hall
why do I smell spaghetti cooking
which was her favorite meal

Why does my cat purr
when there's no one around
why does my dog get anxious
and wants to go outside

Why does she need me so
why can't she let me go
why does she appear in my dreams
and haunt my memories

I guess her goodbye wasn't strong enough
she wants more of my love
lord knows I miss her so much
knowing I'll never find that kind of love again

So I go for a long walk outside
make spaghetti in her honor
spray her perfume in all the rooms
maybe her ghost was all in my mind

Maybe I'm the one who needs her so.

Spirit in your Mirror

I watch you from my side of your mirror
as you go about your morning and night routines
you're always frustrated trying to figure out
what clothes to wear
wondering if this is the day you'll finally fit in
I hear your colorful comments
about your teachers, family, and friends
how depressing life must be
if you're always angry and upset

Every night I watch you toss and turn as you sleep
punching your pillows trying to get comfortable
I project depressing thoughts and images
into your dreams of how you view your life
clocks melting, flowers wilting, endless rainy days
cats cowering, bell towers crumbling, dogs howling in pain
slowly I'll drive you insane

Unbeknownst to you, our hand's touch
as you press them against the glass
our eyes lock for a moment
I peer into your soul
and search for your deepest darkest fears
and use them against you
to cause your nightmares
and make you slowly go insane

I'm a spirit living in your mirror
conjured up by your anger and loneliness
always watching you day and night
as you go on living your life as best as you can
but one day you'll stare into your mirror
scream out in fright
as I reveal your true self to you
which will haunt your dreams for eternity.

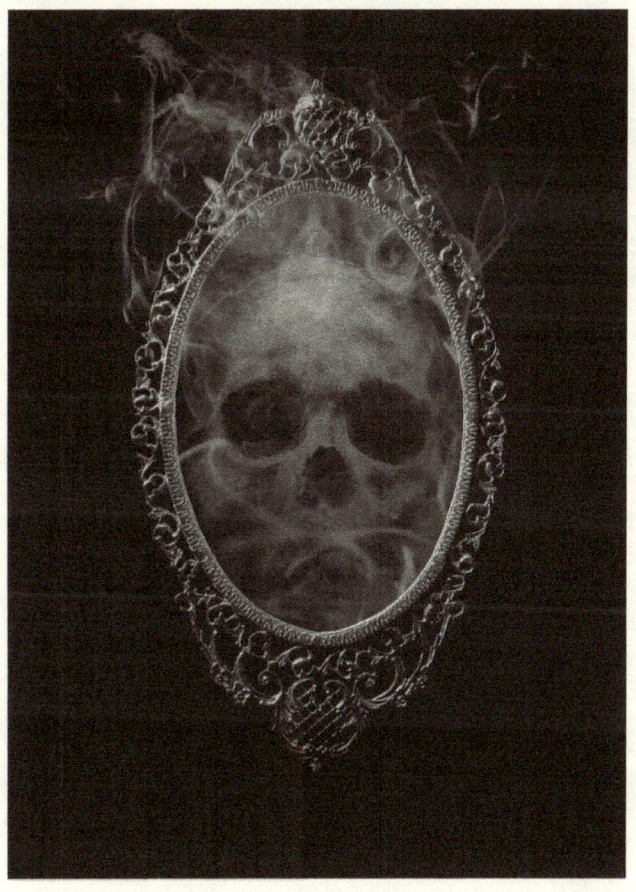

The Taylor's are Moving

"Mama," cries the young girl
"I just heard the Taylors are moving
I don't know what I'm going to do
Sarah's been my best friend since 2012
and the only one who shared her toys with me
I'm going to miss her,"
she hugs her mom tight as tears run down her cheek

"Oh honey, I'm so sorry," her mom says
"think of all the good times you had
playing hopscotch and games
swinging on the swing set
boy, did you give her a fright
on the first night you met her
and you never let her sleep"

"Mama, I'm worried the new tenants
won't be so nice and kind
what if there's no girl my age,"
"oh honey, I won't let that happen
you know I won't allow just anyone to move in
who doesn't have a girl
we'll do what we do best,"

Weeks passed after the Taylor's moved out
the landlord can't figure out why no one is moving in
despite its location in the city and cheap rent
but he doesn't know
there's a ghost of a mom and little girl
protecting their forever home

"Mama," cried the little girl "look outside,"
she leads her mom to the living room window
they peer out to see a family with two young girls
walking up the front lawn
they watch as the father smiles, the mother nods
as the girls run around the yard
"let's make sure they get it, and you can have twice the fun
let's disappear so they can view the house in peace
you'll have plenty of time to play with them
after they move in."

Doppelgänger

I couldn't believe my eyes
when I saw what looked like another me
walking and talking with my friend Kevin
on the opposite side of the street
I ducked out of view
and watched them disappear around the corner
that night Kevin called me
thanking me for the advice that I gave him

Day after day my friends called me
saying they had a wonderful time with me
appreciating that I took the time out of my busy schedule
to spend the day fishing with them or having lunch together
even my sister who lives thirty miles away
was surprised to see me when I showed up at her door
I grew concerned at all the stories they were telling me

A few weeks later, as I was leaving for work
my boss called me his voice a mixture
of anger and disappointment
said not to come in, that I was fired
for deleting months of data and files off the mainframe
I tried to explain that it wasn't me
but he replied they had me on tape
and he had to let me go

I threw down my phone, I was angry and confused
I didn't understand what was going on
then came the texts from my friends
who were now upset at me
saying I was out of line and rude with them
said they never wanted to talk to me again

It all came to a blow a few nights later
as I laid in bed
I was depressed, just wanted a good night's sleep
when there came a knock on my bedroom door
I looked up to see my double standing there
"Who are you," I demanded "what do you want from me,"
my double didn't say a word
to my horror, he began to morph
his skin hung off his bones, his hair was falling out
his eyes were hollow and deep
rotting flesh filled the air as he came towards me

His skeletal arms wrapped around my throat
I started to choke as his grip grew tighter
I stared into his hallowed eyes
trying to find the answer
of my why my twin who never existed
was trying to kill me.

Dinner Time

I was down by the river
skipping rocks in the water
shadows from the trees were growing taller
the sun shone directly into my eyes
I heard the crunching of dead leaves
and a growl that traveled in the wind
I saw the waters began to part
a cold shiver ran up my spine
knew that I was no longer alone
I threw down the rock that was in my hand
and made a beeline straight to my home

I got scratched by twigs and thorns
as I ran from something that I couldn't see
but I could feel it following me
I reached the bottom of the hill
I could see my house with my mama on the porch
she had a worried look on her face
as she was calling me in for dinner
"Mama, I'm almost home," I called out

I was halfway up the hill
when the sky turned dark, a strong wind began to blow
knocked me down to my knees
I saw the lawn chairs and weather vane blowing away
but I kept on, knowing somehow, I had to protect my mama
I sped up and made a lunge onto the porch
and knocked down the door

"Mama, I'm here, come on we need to get out of here,"
I searched all the rooms as glass shattered all around me
but my mama couldn't be found
in the kitchen, our dinner was still on the stove
as I walked back into the living room
there was a scruffy looking man with his dirt on his face
his clothes were soaked
he said "I followed you from the river do you
mind if I stay for dinner,"
he let out a cackle as the house blew apart
then I blacked out

"Chris, It's dinner time," I heard my mama calling me
I awoke on the riverbank with a rock in my hand
"I must have been dreaming," I said
I got up and threw the rock into the water
and headed back home
I picked up my pace
as I heard the waters began to part.

The witches Funeral

There were no mourners
just the townspeople and their curiosity
gathered around the grave of the old woman
who was rumored to be a witch
the preacher opened his bible out of pity
when suddenly there was a frenzy

Dark clouds formed overhead
a ferocious wind began to blow
lightning crawled across the sky
the thunder sounded like an old woman's cackle
the townspeople quivered in fear
as the face of the old woman appeared in the sky

"Why are you here with your sympathy and concern
I know you believed the rumor I was a witch
who practiced dark magic
I told Mabel and Paul fifty years ago
to spread it around town
so you would leave me alone which you did

Truth be told I was a reclusive
who wanted to be left alone
I still want to be left alone
but you're crowding my grave
you've spurned my soul
now I'm going to take my revenge
and live forever with the reputation
of being a witch,"

The townspeople quickly dispersed
as sulfuric acid fell from the sky
burning their skin
crows and vultures swarmed and chased the priest
the old lady had her revenge
soon her tombstone was engraved with the words
A lady in life, a witch in death

Now every time it storms
you can hear the laughing of the old lady
as she gets her revenge on the townspeople.

The girl at the Window

What shall become of me when I turn eighteen
she wonders as she stares out her bedroom window
at her grandmother's garden below
will I become a wildflower that blooms
and meet sailors who'll take me away on their yachts
will I become a southern belle
hosting parties for politicians and influential people
will I become a butterfly and fly away
to a distant land that I don't know the name of
or will I be like the ivy
clinging to the history of my family

She turns away for a moment
maybe my dad already has suitors lined up
having me meet them one at a time
so he can vet them at his leisure
perhaps that's why he gave me that fancy dress last week
only if my mom was still here
she could calm my fears and give me advice
I would ask my grandmother but's she confined to bed
and doesn't say much these days

She goes back to her window and says
"time hasn't been too kind to me
dreams are just illusions
out of reach for a girl like me
I don't know the way of the streets
my dad sheltered me from the world
after my mother died"

Joe Tallarigo

"What I've learned about life
is from the books on my shelves
from Romeo and Juliet, Little Women, and fairy tales
I would like to go out and have my own adventures
but none of my family visits, no friends come calling
I'm a prisoner behind these iron gates
there are days I forget my name
and wish I could disappear from here"

She puts on her new dress, stares into her mirror
the bright blue brings out her eyes
she puts on a record on the phonograph
slow dances alone
dreaming of the day she'll catch some guys eyes
lead her out into the garden and past the iron gates
says "I'll buy you all the pearls and jewels you desire
we'll travel the world and have many adventures
you'll never feel lonely again as he asks her to be his wife,"

As the record ends, reality sets back in
she takes off her dress
and goes back staring out her window
to her grandmother's garden below.

A man with no Name

Once upon a scene
one of loneliness and pouring rain
he sits in a booth at a corner café
with an empty coffee cup
the waitress is busy with other customers
and doesn't notice him
he's a drifter going town to town
making guest appearances in the background

He tries his best to climb the social scene
he has the passion and dedication
but the movie producers say he has a plain face
and will never land a leading role
it breaks his heart
knowing he may never be a big star

But he still dreams of the day he'll see his face
on the cover of magazines
the cameras will focus on him
he waves to his fans as he exits his limousine
then walks the red carpet into his world premiere
he'll smile when he sees his name on the big screen
and gets booked on the late-night talk shows

But he's only a drifter going town to town
when he's out no one gives him a second look
he's just another face in the crowd
he'll never earn a star on the Hollywood Walk of Fame
since he's just a man with no name.

The Hitchhiker

He drove on route twenty-nine
looking for his next victim in the moonlight
runaway teens and out-of-towners
were always ripe for the taking
since no one would miss them
he loved to hear their screams as they put up a fight
he's been at this for ten years and has never been caught

"I'm in luck," he said as his headlights shine on a teenage girl
he slowed down, rolled down the passenger side window
"Do you need a lift?" he asked her
"I need to get to Batesville
since my home life isn't that great,"
"hop on in, I'll be happy to take you," he said
as he drove along, a cold chill ran up his spine
her sandy blond hair, blue eyes, bright smile
reminded him of one of his other victims
but he put it out of his mind

A thick fog rolled in
dark heavy clouds blocked out the moon
his thoughts turned to him dragging her into the woods
she'll scream, he smiles knowing no one can hear her
"you look thirsty, have a drink,"
she said interrupting his thoughts
she offered him her water bottle
"thanks," he said as he takes the water bottle to gain her trust

As he came upon the wooded area of his killing grounds
he slowed down, "we have to get out, the car is out of gas
there's a gas station two miles down the road
we can go together," he said
the girl happily obliged, knowing the poison
she put in the water would soon take effect
and she'd have all the power

He opened the trunk and ordered her to grab the gas can
as she drew near, he gripped her shoulders
she screamed as he led her into the woods
as he tied her up
his eyes got blurry and his legs grew weak
he fell to the ground
the girl untied herself, pulled out a knife, stood over him
"you'll be dead soon, but I have to tell you
my name is Kim, last year you killed my twin
she didn't deserve to die for wanting to run away
I carefully planned my revenge and here I am,"

She looked into his almost dead cold eyes
as she thrust the knife into his stomach
gave it a hard twist, he convulsed
"I'll see you in hell," he hissed as he took his last breath

She waited a few minutes, gave him four hard kicks
then drug his body deep in the woods
to make sure no one would ever find him.

Her Alibi

Keri showed up at my door at seven
with a bottle of wine, said mind if I come in
she was unusually calm as she sat on my couch
"I've been thinking it's sweet you never stopped chasing me
even though I was in love with Brian
but I recently discovered he's been cheating on me
I'm done with him, he left me a note saying he was leaving,"

I excused myself to get two glasses, another plate of chicken
my heart raced with the thought of being with her
I've been in love with her since I was fifteen
I sat back down next to her on the couch
she opened and poured the wine
we raised our glasses as she toasted to new beginnings

As she took a sip, the glass slipped out of her hand
"I'm so sorry," she said as she wiped off her dress
"do you mind if I wash it here?" she asked
"sure," I replied, "let me get you a change of clothes,"
something felt off as I got her a pair of my pajamas
but quickly put it out of my mind
when her eyes locked with mine

Her crimson red lips pressed up to mine
her long dark hair flowed over me
her soft hands explored my body
her green eyes told me she held a secret
but loves fever wouldn't let her talk
I knew she was up to something
why of all nights would she show up at my door

As we got dressed, police sirens filled the air
she got a frightened look in her eyes as they drew near
that's when I put two and two together
a hard knock came at my door
"open up, it's the sheriff, we need to talk," a male voice said

I opened the door to see Sheriff Thomas
with a few deputies as backup
said, "we're here for Keri, an hour ago
we found Brian in his truck, a single gun-shot to his head
the bullet matched a 22 caliber which she has a license for,"

She twitched, looked over at me
as the sheriff put her in cuffs
she knew she almost pulled it off
as he walked her to the doo
I yelled "stop she couldn't have done it
she's been with me all evening
as you can see we had dinner, a glass of wine
and had some fun, if you know what I mean,"

"I see," The sheriff said looking at our dishes
"she's off the hook for now, just don't leave town,"
she sighed, "that was close, why did you stick up for me?"
I said, "I lost you once, didn't want to lose you again
plus, I don't think you'll do great in prison,"

The case went cold
we got married and never talked about the night
when I was her alibi.

Blood Money

Drinking my tea in the parlor
sitting on the rose floral couch
that six generations of Mackay's sat on
every bookshelf is full of journals and diaries
detailing their corruption and backstabbing
but three inches of dust is on the shelves
showing I have no interest in continuing the family business

I feel each family member judging me
peering down at me from their paintings
their eyes and demeanor show
they would do anything for a quick buck
despite being judges, politicians, lawyers, and teachers
they were also swindler's, gamblers, and con-men
preying on those down on their luck
taking their money and last shred of hope

My dad was the first to say he wasn't proud
but his roots and legacy were bound to this town
he was only seven when he began
to take advantage of his friends
he almost died twice by the time he was twenty-four
but on the day I was born he said no more

On my eighteenth birthday
he went to the bank for his redemption
he was withdrawing all the money our family accumulated
so he could give it back to the town
when two masked men burst into the lobby
shot him dead, stole the money
the cops allowed them to make a clean escape

Little did the cops know
I tracked them down and shot them dead
buried their bodies deep in the swamp
my dad was trying to do things right
he didn't deserve to die
neither did they, I just wanted the money
but they wouldn't put down their guns
and wouldn't give me the money

The sins of my family won't be on me
their ghosts can come and torment me
but they won't change my mind
the money doesn't belong to me
for too many lives were destroyed
it's time to make things right

Tonight, at city hall
I'm presenting the town a check for ten million dollars
to invest in the community that my family robbed from
and when I go back home, I'll make one more cup of tea
one last walk through the Mackay mansion
then it'll be going up in flames

It's now midnight I'm boarding a red-eye flight
with one suitcase
as the plane takes off in the sky
I give the town a wave goodbye
I pat my suitcase with one million dollars
that I decided to keep for myself
I am a Mackay after all
it's in my blood to be a swindler and con-man.

Joe Tallarigo

Chapter 6

Fantasy has gone out of Style

Fantasy has gone out of Style

I'm tired of being the knight in shining armor
trying to rescue the princess locked away in a faraway land
I'm done being nice, it hasn't gotten me anywhere in life
so if you're wishing upon a star tonight
that I'll ride in on my white horse
you better change that wish for a while
since fantasy has gone out of style

You stare into your magic mirror
hoping that I'll appear
I hate to break your beautiful smile
by not dancing with you tonight in the fancy ballroom
wanting to show me off to your friends and special guests
but you might as well as hang up your dress
since fantasy has gone out of style

Your mother always told you
there will be a prince to put on your glass slipper
but there's another belief you held true
that a brave knight will slay a dragon
hold his sword up in triumph
you'll run down the stairs of your ivory tower
takes your hero into your arms, get married
but your beliefs are clouded
since fantasy has gone out of style.

T&T (Twisted and Tragic)

She was nineteen, out on her own for the first time
she got blinded and misguided by the bright city lights
a group of rowdy people took her off the streets
she's been living it up these past few weeks
while her parents patiently wait to hear from their baby girl

The young shy country girl
her parents wouldn't recognize
she's been introduced to a whole new world
something she believed she'd never be exposed to
now she's a walking time bomb ready to explode
she's wasted, high, has no desire to work
or get ahead in life, it's twisted and tragic
the road she's going down

She chases white lines with strangers in fancy cars
staying out until dawn to get her highs
the devil has her in his sights to rule over her life

The young shy country girl
her parents wouldn't recognize
she's been introduced to a whole new world
something she believed she'd never be exposed to
now she's a walking time bomb ready to explode
she's wasted, high, has no desire to work
or get ahead in life, it's twisted and tragic
the road she's going down

The once straight "A" student who held so much promise
is quickly sinking, it's twisted and tragic
she ever got this way.

Long Night

He got up in front of the congregation
said, before I get baptized next week
I want to share the story of my long night that led me here

It was my usual Friday night
drinking at the bar with my friends
we were laughing and getting loud
I didn't pay attention to how many drinks I consumed
Abby begged me not to drive
that she would take me home
but I assured her I was sober enough to drive

Somewhere along the way, I lost control of my steering
I was swerving back and forth across the double yellow lines
and smashed into two bright headlights
I heard the crunching of metal, the screams
I lost consciousness, found myself in a dark abyss
I was surrounded by hot flames shooting into the air
I heard demons growling
and the mournful cries of the unsaved

I looked down to discover that I was a spirit
there was no peaceful feeling
as I watched the other unsaved souls swirl all around me
wondering when I'd get pulled in
with no chance of redemption

As I waited for my fate, it grew darker and hotter
the growling grew deeper
the mournful cries brought me down to my knees
then a bright light appeared before me
there stood a man, a woman, two boys
asking me why, why, why, they had to die
oh God, what have I done, I'm so sorry, I cried out
they faded as a ten-foot shadow came towards me
I felt two hands grip my shoulder
I closed my eyes, ready to accept my fate
but as time passed, I felt myself flying
through space and time

I soon found myself hovering over my body
lying in a hospital bed connected to wires and machines
I lowered myself into my body and jolted awake
I gasped for breath
the nurse took a step back in shock
said, "you gave us a scare"
I broke down and cried
and declared I'm not drinking anymore
I have a lot of repenting to do

I began reading the bible, found the way and the truth
but it still weighs heavily on my mind
I took four innocent lives
I know nothing can bring them back
all I can do is ask for forgiveness
and live a good life
spreading the message of the gospel to others.

Monster amongst Them

He lived amongst his neighbors
giving them his time and money
spreading hope and joy throughout the community
little did they know, he held a deep secret
that he was the one they've been searching for

A week before Halloween in 1999
two young boys were walking their dog on Hollister Avenue
when he approached them
said he was having car trouble and needed help

He led them down to the river
tied them and the dog up, then killed them
he showed no remorse as he disposed of their lifeless bodies
in the muddy water

Since no one saw him commit the crime
he went on living his life
he married a strawberry blond accountant
fathered a daughter and son
became a member of the PTA
using his charisma and charm
he became a driving force of raising money
for school trips and plays

He kept his secret hidden well
that was until his daughter and son
turned the age of the two brothers
he soon became agitated, saw them in his dreams
heard their pleas and screams every night

He fought his guilt
but began finding wet footprints and pieces of rope
around his house
he grew paranoid and distraught
his wife grew concerned for his welfare
and was confused why he was acting this way

It wasn't until one night when the dog cornered him
who was growling nonstop
that he finally broke down and went straight to the police
he led a few officers to the river
told them he was the one who killed the brothers and dog
he got on his knees, put his hands behind his head
he was relieved to put his guilt to rest

As the cops pulled away
the spirits of the brothers and their dog
rose from the river and flew away into the starry sky
for they were now at peace.

High Society

Suit and ties mean nothing to me
look at all the lying politicians in Washington, D.C.
smiling in front of all the cameras
making empty promises on tv
while bankers, Wall Street, and CEO's
line their pockets with silver and gold
smoking their fancy cigars, drinking high priced wine
as they fly all over the world in their gulf streams

You can keep your high society
as you keep robbing us blind
banks keep adding on fees
taking more of our money from our thirty-hour paycheck
they tell us not to be greedy
but when they lose money
they cry and throw tantrums
saying you need to keep us afloat
we need to buy new boats
and keep up our way of living

Many are living paycheck to paycheck
can't even afford their rent
yet no bailouts are being given
to the hard-working men and women
if it wasn't for us
there would be no rich CEO'S
and when we ask for raises
they say get another job
don't spend more than you can afford

You can keep your high society
as you keep robbing us blind
banks keep adding on fees
taking more of our money from our thirty-hour paycheck
they tell us not to be greedy
but when they lose money
they cry and throw tantrums
saying you need to keep us afloat
we need to buy new boats
and keep up our way of living

There are three-dollar fees to withdraw
our money from ATM's
ten-dollar fees to pay bills by phone
five-dollar fees to pay by check
they squeeze out our last nickels and dimes
so they can host fancy parties, buy two more houses
and give themselves raises

You can keep your high society
as you keep robbing us blind
banks keep adding on fees
taking more of our money from our thirty-hour paycheck
they tell us not to be greedy
but when they lose money
they cry and throw tantrums
saying you need to keep us afloat
we need to buy new boats
and keep up our way of living.

Changing World

Some days I feel tired and weak
I just want to stay in bed
where I feel content in my dreams
the world is changing at a fast pace
no matter how hard I try to keep up
I feel like I'm always two steps behind

What is truth, what is lies
the lines are getting blurred
anger and resentment seem to be the flavors of the day
I've learned through my ire and rage
that finding happiness and peace
can only come from within

I don't care about politics
I'm not bounded by either side
most politicians have crooked tongues
throw millions of dollars into their circus
when that money could help so many

What is truth, what is lies
the lines are getting blurred
anger and resentment seem to be the flavors of the day
I've learned through my ire and rage
that finding happiness and peace
can only come from within

Climate change, cancel culture, erasing history
defund the police, taking shows off the air
are the talks of the town
with the political division so bad there's no middle ground
but in the times of this despair
I find solace in my bible
knowing that God is still in control
and will one day take back His world

What is truth, what is lies
the lines are getting blurred
anger and resentment seem to be the flavors of the day
I've learned through my ire and rage
that finding happiness and peace
can only come from within.

Faces in our Phones

Do you ever feel alone walking down the street
even though you're amongst a crowd
do you ever feel like you're talking to yourself
even though you're with your friends
do your kids play outside, ride their bikes
or are they in their rooms
like everyone else with their face in their phones

Constant news updates, sports scores
emailing coworkers from a train
must update the world
about the trendy new restaurant you're eating at
posting pictures of the delicious food
we need to complain about the rain
getting tickets to the hottest play
announcing you got a new car
everyone feels like a big star
with their constant updates
but we're just alone
with our faces in our phones

We text during movies or watching tv
post photos of our kids and pets
make vague posts about past regrets
searching for a new dish to make
must go toe to toe
with your friends, family, and strangers
so you don't feel like an average Joe

We take quizzes and play games
buy and sell items online
we announce to the world
about our new relationship
update everyone on your weight-loss journey
send prayers to those who need it the most
we check-in at the events we're attending
everyone feels like a big star
with their constant updates
but we're just alone
with our faces in our phones

How can we be with friends and family
be amongst a crowd
yet feel so alone
when we have our faces in our phones.

Broken Dreams

Standing at the edge of the state line
as the sun sets in the west
guess he's tired as I am
I peer back at my hometown one last time
not having the strength to say goodbye
the wind is blowing in my face
don't know where I'm heading
I thought being older meant being wiser
but that doesn't seem to be the case

All my planning has only brought broken dreams
every time life seems to go my way
the devil comes out to play
leaves behind sadness and pain
there were times I was tempted to give in
but I got down on my knees, asked God to forgive my sins
and lead me away from this land of broken dreams

I've been walking through this darkness and uncertainty
my boots full of dirt and mud
with holes in my soles, life's a hard journey
that only gets harder as I get two steps ahead

All my planning has only brought broken dreams
every time life seems to go my way
the devil comes out to play
leaves behind sadness and pain
there were times I was tempted to give in
but I got down on my knees, asked God to forgive my sins
and lead me away from this land of broken dreams.

Write it out

We get mad and upset
want to throw and break things
punch a hole in the wall
we blow our top, scream, and shout
so loud that the world can hear us
when we should just pick up a pen
take a piece of paper
and write our frustrations out

We fall in love, head over heels
want to hold their hand
tell them our life story
take them to fancy restaurants
layout beneath the stars
but slow it down a bit
since we just met them
pick up a pen, take a piece of paper
and write our feelings out

Life throws us curves
makes us question our beliefs
we don't know where to begin
to figure out what is truth
and what is fiction
it'll cause some friction as we untangle it
the bottom may fall out
pick up a pen, take a piece of paper
and write our philosophies out.

Staying Home

I used to believe that I had to be part of the crowd
so I wouldn't feel I missed out on the fun
that I was cool to be part of the social scene
and that I would have regrets if I missed out on an event
that I'd be hanging out with friends or meeting someone new
and was part of something bigger than me

Now I find myself aligned with those
who choose to stay home and be recluse
I'm catching up on my favorite shows
finishing books that I started years ago
I'm more relaxed and even-tempered
since I no longer rush out of the house
feeling like I must be the first to arrive
to avoid the hassle of big crowds

I used to attend every concert
made my way to the front of the stage
live music was my addiction
hearing the songs in person was the cure
but as the last note was being played
I was already looking forward to the next show

Now I find myself aligned with those
who choose to stay home and be recluse
I'm catching up on my favorite shows
finishing books that I started years ago
I'm more relaxed and even-tempered
since I no longer rush out of the house
feeling like I must be the first to arrive
to avoid the hassle of big crowds

Every day at my job I gave it my all
but found it caused burnout
I believed if I had my life together
it would prevent the rug from being
pulled out from under me
but reality hit me like a ton of bricks

Now I find myself aligned with those
who choose to stay home and be recluse
I'm catching up on my favorite shows
finishing books that I started years ago
I'm more relaxed and even-tempered
since I no longer rush out of the house
feeling like I must be the first to arrive
to avoid the hassle of big crowds.

Unwelcomed

Your eyes stare off in the distance
focusing on something else besides me
but that's nothing new
you never hear a word I say
I can feel a big change coming
I'm positive that I won't be part of it
I'll be unwelcomed
in this new stage of your life

I won't slam the door when I leave
I'll come to realize you were always cold-hearted
that all along you never wanted me in your world
you were always playing with my feelings
I'm not surprised this came out of nowhere
you always kept me in the dark
with the plans you made for us
it's just my luck I'm now unwelcomed for good

I should have seen it coming
I knew our love was never strong
but deep down I wanted to hang on
though my friends and family told me to leave
but I wanted a chance to see
if I could change your cold-hearted ways
I wanted to make you happy, bring you joy
not once did you accept my love
now you're moving on without me
making me feel even more unwelcomed in your life

I won't slam the door when I leave
I've come to realize you were always cold-hearted
that all along you never wanted me in your world
you were always playing with my feelings
I'm not surprised this came out of nowhere
you always kept me in the dark
with the plans you made for us
it's just my luck I'm now unwelcomed for good.

The tears come Falling

Why can't we laugh and talk like the good ole days
why does it hurt so much to even touch you
the words I can't form to say I'm sorry, I love you

The tears come falling
separating you from me
sweeping my feelings down love's memory
I want to walk away with a smile on my face
but the tears come falling

I can't stop crying
knowing soon you'll be with another
you were my only true love
how can I go when my sunshine has gone away
to light up someone else's life

The tears come falling
separating you from me
sweeping my feelings down love's memory
I want to walk away with a smile on my face
but the tears come falling

Breaking down is all I can do
when the world turns it back on me
and love has gone astray
there'll be a lot of lonely nights and days
I'm crying over our last kiss
knowing you're now with another man.

She didn't even blink

She caught me off guard
when she said, "I have to tell you something
I won't be able to rest until I get this off my chest,"
but not one word was spoken at dinner
I grew nervous with each bite we took
finally, as she took her last bite
she looked me straight in the eyes
she didn't even blink as she said

"I've been seeing Chris, it began at the office
we made love on our business trips
I lied about my intentions
when I went to Maryland and Tennessee
that was just a cover for our love affair
I'm leaving tonight with him
you can't change my mind
this is what I want for me,"

I could only watch with tears in my eyes
as she put the dinner plates in the sink
then walked to the basement
came back up with the suitcases
we bought for our honeymoon
she walked into our bedroom
packed her clothes, her jewelry
but left behind her wedding ring
she didn't even blink
when she walked out the door
with her words replaying in my mind

"I've been seeing Chris, it began at the office
we made love on our business trips
I lied about my intentions
when I went to Maryland and Tennessee
that was just a cover for our love affair
I'm leaving tonight with him
you can't change my mind
this is what I want for me,"

A few months later, I ran into one of her best friends
she told me she attended their wedding
and she didn't even blink when she said, "I do."

A woman's Plea

She stared at me with desperate eyes
how many times have you ignored me through the years
why can't you see I need some passion in my nights
what's happened to the spark we shared
where are the surprises you gave me
when we first started dating
I remember there was a time you couldn't wait to get home
now I feel all alone
but there's an old flame that's been asking about me

Can you at least listen to me
am I not as fun as I used to be
have I been working too hard on the things
that you no longer want
have I been a fool to think I could keep you happy
is there someone else I can't compete with
does she secretly give you what you need
am I going to be shown the door

While you decide what to say
try to recall the first day we met
how you made me feel in front of our friends
was that real or just an act to make yourself look good
did you plan this life all along
dragging me along in your childish games
well I have more to say

Somewhere along our journey
something inside of you must have died
why else would you treat me this way
or have you been miserable all along
if you want me to go just say so
we have our own lives to live
I can't go on without having passion in my nights
I still have a fire inside of me that needs to be satisfied.

Fool Moon

It's that time of the month again
when men's mouths speak faster
than what their brain can control
they drive their woman crazy
make them cry for a week or two
it's not their fault
blame it on the fool moon

Men don't think things through
all they want to do is drink
act ten feet tall and bulletproof
crushing cans against their heads
to impress the girls in the bars
they sing karaoke to one or two
it's not their fault
blame it on the fool moon

They put the pedal to the metal
drive as fast as they can down the double yellow lines
wanting to fly like the wind, but they'll never get far
even if they are number one or two
it's not their fault
blame it on the fool moon

Fool moons drive men crazy
even the most faithful of men get pulled in
wild and crazy ideas get put into their heads
must act out on them
it's always been this way since one or two B.C.
it's not their fault
blame it on the fool moon.

She's got the law looking for Me

I made the mistake of forgetting our anniversary
now she's got the law looking for me

All last week she dropped hints
something big was coming up
but being a guy I focused on other things
she even hinted at a new diamond ring
mentioned something about exchanging our vows again
I somehow only caught the tail end of that conversation
because I'm now on the run

I made the mistake of forgetting our anniversary
now she's got the law looking for me

Her mother called me, insisted she would keep the kids
I said sure, I would drop them off by six
thought I had an all-clear to go fishing
since my wife also made plans
what an earful I got when she called me
and asked where I was

As I was fishing at the lake, I heard the police sirens
knew I had only minutes to make my escape
as I got in my truck, my heart sank
knew I had let my wife down
and for the rest of my life I'll be making it up to her
she's going to be my judge and jury
since I made the mistake of forgetting our anniversary.

Dirty words to Men

Turn off the tv it's time to spring clean
laundry needs to get done
dishes aren't going to wash themselves
the grass needs mowing
don't forget my mother is coming to town this weekend
you can't hang out with your friends
these are dirty words to men

Lockouts are looming in football and baseball
hey honey, when are we going to expand our family tree
can you fill up my car, it's past empty
also, can I have fifty dollars there's a dress I need
and you still can't hang out with your friends
these are dirty words to men

Does this new dress make me look fat
your boss called he needs you to work all weekend
Monday is Valentine's day, did you make the reservations
at the new five-star restaurant everyone is talking about
and you still can't hang out with your friends
these are dirty words to men

To make us happy, say
I bought you some tickets on the fifty-yard line
invite your friends over for poker
my mother is staying in a hotel
here are bows and arrows for hunting
honey, don't look at me like that
you know your mother is always welcome here.

Front Door

I fumble for my keys as I wave goodbye to my friend
who was driving away
I told him I was okay, I must do this on my own
though I can barely see through my tear-stained eyes
with my heart breaking in two as I stand in front of our
front door

It's the first time in forty years you're not here to greet me
I take a deep breath, say a brief prayer
as I unlock the door
I hope I can handle being alone
with the memories we made behind this front door

I still see the joy on your face
when I surprised you with this place
it was supposed to be our palace
I still feel you in my arms
as I carried you over the threshold
when we were twenty-four, now I'm about to enter alone

It's the first time in forty years you're not here to greet me
I take a deep breath, say a brief prayer
as I unlock the door
I hope I can handle being alone
with the memories we made behind this front door

I kissed you here goodbye every morning
as I headed off to work
you met here every night with another kiss to say hello
hand in hand we walked to the kitchen
to eat dinner together.

He doesn't play that song Anymore

He wrote Emily's song on a sultry July night
back in 1983 on his front porch swing
he first played it for her on their wedding day in 1984
every night before bed he pulled out his guitar
serenaded her as she brushed her hair
she would smile and thank him for the song
he wrote just for her

One January day in 1987 he got a call
that she wasn't coming home
a four-car pileup with a semi-truck
his guitar has stayed in the closet
he no longer plays the chords
to the song that brought her so much joy
it makes him sad to be in this room

He recalls that sultry July night
sitting on his front porch swing
with his guitar, pen, and paper
smiling as he thought about Emily
the girl he was about to marry
he was on top of the world
as he wrote down the final word and chord
he couldn't wait to play it for her on their wedding day
she cried, gave him a big hug
now he wishes he could go back in time

One January day in 1987 he got a call
that she wasn't coming home
a four-car pileup with a semi-truck
his guitar has stayed in the closet
he no longer plays the chords
to the song that brought her so much joy
it makes him sad to be in this room.

Joe Tallarigo

You would have wanted That

Friday night, a new set of digits on a napkin
slipped to me by the waitress
she said cowboy call me sometime
gave me a wink, moved on to her other tables
I looked down at my wedding band
drank the last of my whiskey
wondering why I felt so guilty

You would have wanted that
you would want me to call her
but I haven't moved on
though it's been four years
through my sorrows and tears
I seem to be tied to my wedding band
my love for you is still burning and can't be put out

I went home, looked through our photos
then walked out to the patio
looked up at the night sky
questioned why we weren't so lucky
to be the ones to have it all
I sighed, went to our bedroom to lie down
felt the emptiness on your side of the bed
had me a good cry
I knew what I had to do

I picked up the phone, called the waitress
we went out the next night
had a great time
maybe in a few weeks
I'll be ready to date again.

I don't want to wake Up

I feel your arms around me holding me tight
so I can't get up and leave for work
I look over at you
your radiant smile brightens the room more than the sun
it feels like the first few years when we were married
not having a care in the world
I'm ready for another long trip to the coast

I don't want to wake up from this dream
it's been seven years but still feels like yesterday
that I said goodbye to you and placed roses on your grave
life wasn't supposed to turn out like this
there's so much I miss
but here you are with me again
and I don't want to wake up

The pain and loneliness tore through my heart
people don't see what I'm feeling
they don't know I cry a few times a day
when I smile and laugh another piece of me dies
there are times I pray to the devil to end my hell on Earth
but now that you're back with me

I don't want to wake up from this dream
it's been seven years but still feels like yesterday
that I said goodbye to you and placed roses on your grave
life wasn't supposed to turn out like this
there's so much I miss
but here you are with me again
and I don't want to wake up

Joe Tallarigo

>The alarm clock is now ringing
>the sunlight is warming my face
>I just want to fade away
>to stay in this dream forever
>so I can be with you again.

Last night of Summer

It's our last night of summer together around the bonfire
roasting marshmallows on sticks
out here in the middle of Kentucky
underneath the black velvet sky
with millions of stars lighting up the night
the flames warm our skin
I'll miss having you around
the chill of an early fall came calling
and you must leave town at tomorrow's sunrise

I'm not ready for you to leave
who's going to explore the caves, and creeks with me
who's going to laugh when I get spooked by owls or bats
or help me catch fireflies in a jar
then release them into the night
as we make a wish upon a shooting star
who's going to help me build a snowman
or snuggle with me by the fireplace
with a cup of hot chocolate
as the snow falls gently outside

I know it's your choice to go to college in Boston
and want to explore the world
you've outgrown your country roots
once you get settled in, I'll come up and visit
you can show me around the city
and I can meet your new friends

My heart is melting like the marshmallows
as I hear the lonesome whistle moan in the distance
that'll be your ride as I'm still sleeping
dreaming of all the fun we had through the years
as you look out your passenger window
at the houses, stores, rivers, and woods
we visited and hung out in
and with each mile farther up the line, you go
you'll question how time flew by and you'll cry

I hope one day you'll put your roots down here again
so we can have bonfires in the summer
feel the warmth of the flames on our skin
as we roast marshmallows, we'll catch fireflies in a jar
and release them into the night
as we make wishes upon a shooting star.

Are you coming Home

Yellow and orange leaves swirl in the wind
blowing across the dead grass
taking away the summer memories we made
gray clouds are moving in
with a threat of rain or snow
and a long-lasting heartache on the horizon

Are you coming home, are you all alone
where did you go, do you still want me
can I send you money
it's not right leaving me in the cold
are you coming home

I can still feel the sand on my skin
and hear the waves crashing on the shore
as we talked about our horizons
where the sun would rise and set in our lives
thinking we had something special
I thought we would fly

Are you coming home, are you all alone
where did you go, do you still want me
can I send you money
it's not right leaving me in the cold
are you coming home

Outside, snow is falling
inside, no one can see my tears of ice
or hear the question in my heart
are you coming home?

Southern Rain

Walking the back roads of Montgomery
through the muck and the mud
as the southern rain pours down on me
the reflections I see of myself in the puddles
are ones I don't like to see
I'm a man who's sad and lonely
but I'm not looking for any company

I wave on the cars who slow down
it's only four miles to the next town
I don't want their smiles to turn into frowns
when they ask me why I'm walking in the rain
I could refrain from answering, but here's the answer
I'm trying to drown this heartache, ease this pain
in this drenching southern rain

I'm not the one to kiss and tell
but she was no southern bell
our passion was hot and steamy
like any given August day
our love flames shone all day and night
we quickly burnt through both ends of the candle
we couldn't handle being lovers anymore
she wouldn't say if we could remain friends
so I walked out her door with my pride
without telling her goodbye
I'm going to miss running my hands
through her fiery red hair
while staring passionately into her dark green eyes

So I'm taking the time to clear my head
on the Montgomery back roads
admiring each pine cone hanging firmly from the fir trees
I wonder if they feel sad or pain
when they know it's time to let go
or do they want to hold on for a little longer
do we as humans let go too soon
especially when love is on the line

Southern rain pours down on me
as I walk the back roads of Montgomery
as I try to drown this heartache and ease my pain.

No girl under my apple Tree

No girl is waiting for me
under my apple tree
no girl of my dreams to take me away
no girl to make a home with
no girl to watch the sunset with
no girl to share a moonlight kiss with

There are no girls around
just apples on the ground
there's no love to be found
just dark clouds blocking out the sun

I wish I was lying in a girl's arm
telling her my hopes and dreams
she'd say baby we'll make them all come true
we'll take it one day at a time, you'll see
but no girl is waiting for me
under my apple tree

There are no girls around
just apples on the ground
there's no love to be found
just dark clouds blocking out the sun

It's another lonely night with my guitar
coming up with a song for a special someone
but she's nowhere to be found
there's an emptiness in my heart
and apples on the ground.

Just when the sun started to shine Again

Just when the sun started to shine again
and the roses bloomed
I even had a dollar to my name
to have a good time
you came blowing back into town
to spread your misery around

The familiar gloomy clouds hang overhead
you must have heard I was happy
you always had a way to rain on my parade
there was always lightning in your eyes
I believe you're an energy vampire
to drain all my happiness away

Just when I thought you went away for good
you showed up at my door
now I'm taking three steps back
falling back into your old traps
you laid out for me
woe is me, I'll never be free

You had me oppressed in your sourness
I could barely function as a person
I always felt catatonic
but by the end of our fourth year together
I finally found the strength to kick you out of the house
and told you never to return

Yet, here you are again
the dogs are howling, clawing to escape
the rivers are running backward
the birds have flown away
replaced by vultures circling overhead
all the store owners have boarded up their shops
that should be enough hints you're not wanted here

Just when the sun started to shine again
and the roses bloom
I even had a dollar to my name
to have a good time
you came blowing back into town
to spread your misery around.

I want to be Alone

Don't turn on the lights
don't cheer me up
I want to drown in my sorrows
my heart is breaking
it will take more than duct tape
to mend my life back together
I don't feel alive
I'm cold as a tombstone
with the date you told me goodbye
carved into my heart

I want to be alone
in the dark, I'll cry
I'll count each tear, there's no reason to go on
you were my only light in this gloomy world
the only one who saw the good in me
now I'm back at the bottom
where I swore I'd never go again
I'm cold as a tombstone
with the date you told me goodbye
carved into my heart

I don't want to sleep
I don't want to eat
can't walk the city streets
without being reminded of the good times we had
I'll be at the railroad tracks
watching the trains roll by until the sun rises
I'm cold as a tombstone
with the date you told me goodbye
carved into my heart

I want to be alone
deep in the woods
with the wolves and the bears
I can't stand love or romance anymore
especially watching cheerful couples on tv
since you walked out my door
I'm not ready to jump back in
I'm cold as a tombstone
with the date you told me goodbye
carved into my heart.

I don't care Anymore

Let me melt in the pouring rain
let the wind take me away
I'm tired of this stalemate
I honestly hope we walk away
never to speak to each other again
I already have one foot out the door
because I don't care anymore

I'm tired of pretending
I'm only suppressing my happiness
I should leave and not shed any tears
I don't want to misrepresent
we might reconcile
when I don't care anymore

I don't care anymore
I have no more dangs to give
please leave me alone
there's not much more I can say
I won't show any emotion
since I'm done with our devotion

Let me melt in the pouring rain
let the wind take me away
I'm tired of this stalemate
I honestly hope we walk away
never to speak to each other again
I already have one foot out the door
because I don't care anymore.

Was I wrong

Was I wrong to sing you my song
on that June day on your front porch swing
then showed up a few days later at your door
with a bouquet asking you for a date
to the county fair

Was I wrong to win you a few teddy bears
to go on a ride in the tunnel of love
though we're just friends
then I took you to the top of the Ferris wheel
to overlook the city

Was I wrong to hold you close
when we were dancing
was I a fool to say we had a song
to get my hopes up too high
that maybe we might fall in love

Was I wrong to rope the moon and stars
when I gave you my class ring
asked you to go steady
when you weren't ready as I was
should I give you more time

Was I wrong to give you the things you wanted
since it was your heart that told me
it wanted all these things
when it was next to mine.

Ode to Hank Williams and Vern Gosdin

If it wasn't for Hank Williams and Vern Gosdin
I wouldn't have written such sad songs

In 2003, I bought Vern Gosdin's greatest hits cd
and listened to it nonstop
"Do You Believe Me Now" sent shivers up my spine
and tore through my soul in a way I never felt before
and to this day it still makes me cry

I found Hank Williams double cd at my aunt's house
I borrowed it and listened to every song
"Ramblin' Man" and "Lost Highway"
captured my fancy, I never heard such sorrow and despair
made me want to dig down deep in my soul
see how dark and depressing I could go
would I survive going into the rabbit hole
that I was going down to write these poems

It's been a journey, one of heartache and pain
long nights alone in the dark
trying to find the right words
that will tear into your soul
make you feel the sadness and despair
that I was experiencing at the time writing these poems

Hank Williams and Vern Gosdin sure could sing a song
make you feel every word they sang
they sure don't make sad songs like that anymore
it seems like today's broken hearts
don't hurt as much as it did back then
people today seem to walk away with a smile on their face
and hop into a new relationship on the same day.

Chapter Seven

My paranormal Experiences

(These poems are based on my experiences with the paranormal from 1988-2020)

Ghost on my Wall
(1988)

I was three years old, waking up to the sun shining
my younger brother was sleeping soundly in his crib
our bedroom was in the dining room
which was next to my parents' bedroom
I was deciding if I wanted to eat or stay in bed
as I looked toward the kitchen, my eyes widened
and I quickly pulled the covers over my head

On the wall surrounding the light switch
there was a shadow shaped like a Pac-man ghost
with two circle eyes and oval mouth
I couldn't believe what I saw
I peeked out from under my covers
the shadow was still there

I went back under my covers and fell asleep
I had a feeling the shadow wasn't going to hurt me
it just appeared to let me know
that it would watch me from then on

I awoke later that morning
the shadow disappeared
I never saw it again
but I had many more paranormal experiences
after he first appeared to me.

My Nightmares

I was three years old, only knee-high
making my way around the room
at a family party, a phone rang
no one seemed to notice or care
so I picked up the phone, said hello
to my horror on the other end of the line
was heavy breathing, then a demonic growl

When I was four years old
I was outside playing in the leaves
with my older sister
when I noticed shadows of druids
on the apartment wall next to us
they were chanting something sinister
I felt that we would be in danger if they noticed us

When I was five years old
wild animals inhabited my backyard
I was too scared to go outside
to play on my swing-set
then when I was seven
I saw a green U.F.O. hovering in the night sky
just outside my living room window

When I was thirteen I moved out of the house
soon after I began having nightmares about the house
I found myself standing at the bottom of the stairwell
that led to the bedroom on the second floor
but fear paralyzed me to even take one step up
because I felt an evil presence waiting in the dark for me
I had the same dream dozens of times
only once did I face my fears and go up the stairs

I'm still curious to know
why I had such wicked dreams
and what's been haunting me
since I was three years old
but the city tore down my childhood home
I may never know who or what it was.

The stairwell to my Bedroom

Nightmare Before Easter (1990's)

It was two A.M.
I was returning to bed after a trip to the bathroom
when I saw my brother in my room
he gave me a scare as he was just standing there
it was like he was in a trance
he didn't say a word to me
I chose to go back to sleep
as if everything was normal

The next morning as we were getting dressed
he went downstairs
upset that he couldn't find his dress pants
our mom went upstairs
looked and tore apart his closet
knowing she hung up the day before
but she couldn't find them either

A week later she was doing laundry in the basement
as she was pulling clothes out of the dirty clothes basket
she was shocked to find his pants crumpled up
at the very bottom underneath the other clothes
we were all stumped how they got there

A few weeks later she revealed to us

the night before Easter she woke up at 1:50 A.M.
to see dark shadows that she described as large dark birds
swirling above her
then they flew through the ceiling
into my brother's bedroom.

Devil in the Sky (1995)

I was ten years old
sitting on the steps of Radel's Funeral Home
wishing my friends were home so we could play
I looked up at the bright blue sky
to my shock and surprise
there was a cloud shaped like the devil's face

I couldn't look away
felt myself being slowly put into a trance
filling up with anger and rage
as if I was being possessed from the cloud
shaped like the devil's face

I walked home feeling weird
I would become apprehensive
anytime I saw the color red
one Sunday in June I went to church with my dad
the carpet was bright red
as soon as I walked in, I became feverish and apprehensive
I wanted to leave right away
for I didn't like what I was feeling

I was miserable that whole summer
trying to find a way to shake off the devil
and cure me of his oppression
evil was not in my blood
I was a child of God
he had no right to be in my soul
but I had no answers on how to cure myself

Joe Tallarigo

As that summer turned into fall
I felt like my old self
seeing the color red no longer made me feel apprehensive
by winter I was back to normal
but to this day I wonder why
the cloud was shaped like the devil's face.

I'm a Conduit
(July 2002-Present)

I'm a conduit for those who passed on
the dearly departed reach out to me
through words or images
they tell me their stories
what they were like in this life
telling me specific names or events
so when I reach out to their loved ones
they will have confirmation that their relative or friend
did indeed visit me from the other side

Some have unfinished business
have urgent warnings of danger
others want to let their family they are still around
some are lonely and just want to talk
I respond to them through telepathy
so they can hear me
and we get on the same page

I discovered this gift in July 2002
when I was seventeen
since then it comes and goes
and when the feeling is strong, I can't resist
I open the door to the spiritual world
because I know they have something to say
it might be a lot or not much at all
but it's important for their loved ones
to receive the message

My mom and aunt Sue
have visited me in my dreams
to check in on me and give me messages
sometimes they bring me to tears
because I feel they still want to be here
to be part of our world again
with family and friends

I'm a conduit for those who passed on
the dearly departed reach out to me
through words or images
they tell me their stories
what they were like in this life
telling me specific names or events
so when I reach out to their loved ones
they will have confirmation that their relative or friend
did indeed visit me from the other side.

My Cousin's House (2014)

I walked up the darkened staircase of my cousin's house
the air was thick and heavy when I got to the second floor
as I made my way into the room on the left, I stopped
a small bright circular light moved in a circle on the floor
as if someone was on the ceiling shining a flashlight
I only had my camera, so I know it couldn't have been me
I then took a photo of the room and captured a green orb

Whoosh! A strong icy wind blew past me
making the hair on my arms stand up
goosebumps formed all over my body
I called down to my cousin and dad
they rushed up to where I was
they too felt the chilly air
despite that it was mid-July, and she had no central air
we couldn't rationalize what we were feeling

I walked to the bedroom on the right
as I took pictures with my camera flash
I could see ectoplasm floating in the air
after each photo, I reviewed them
one photo showed what looked like it was snowing
with white strands fell from the ceiling to the floor
then the next photo there was nothing there

I kept calm as I tried to figure out
what I was seeing and feeling
I went in as a skeptic but came out as a believer
since I heard other ghost hunters on tv
describe the same electric charge they feel
when a ghost comes near them.

Get me out of Here
(2017)

"I don't belong here, I don't belong here,"
I say to myself as I pace back and forth
in the living room of my childhood home
I look out the front and back window
wondering how I'm going to get out
aware that it was torn down in 2014
though I'd give anything to stay here
I'm painfully aware that I'm in a dream

I don't believe here, I need to wake up
I keep repeating these words
trying to stay calm
I look at the couch and get an idea
I lay down and close my eyes tight
I count to ten and open my eyes
but to my disappointment, I'm still in the living room
I get up to walk to the front window
looking for anyone who can help me get out

Seeing no one I get back on my couch
I want to give it another try to get out of this dream
knowing I can't stay here
I want to return to my current house
I close my eyes and count to ten
I open my eyes to find myself still in the living room
I start to wonder if I was transported to an alternate reality
where I could stay forever in my childhood home

No, no, no, this can't be
of course, I'd give anything to stay here
but I don't want to stay in this reality
if my family and friends can't be with me
so I close my eyes once more
and focus on my current house
this time I feel myself floating through time and space
I feel myself going back into my body and jolt awake
to find that I'm back in my bed in my present house.

Joe Tallarigo

Feeling of Dread
(2019)

I have a gut feeling, a feeling I haven't felt since 2009
the winds of change are blowing in
I hate this feeling that my stable life may unravel
and I won't be able to control the narrative
I'm lost and confused about what to do
my life is finally heading in the right direction
and don't want to go through hell again

I'm not willing to give up the progress I've made
I worked too hard with a lot of sweat and long nights
to have it change again in an instant
I can't shake this feeling that it'll explode in my face
like it did a decade ago

I could use a sign that everything will be all right
as I walk through this heaviness and darkness
I know I must keep growing and not stay stagnant
I hope this is part of God's plan
and that my life will even be more blessed
unless I mess it up with my stubbornness

I'm in the dark of what's coming
I hope I don't burn the wrong bridges
and let down the people I love the most
I hate change
but I could be better off in the long run
I need the faith of the mustard seed
and let the storm unleash its fury.

Sitting in the Dark
(2019)

I won't sit in the dark
when the shadow man appears again
I will jump into the flames
of his cat and mouse games
I'll put up a stronger fight
so he won't bring me more pain and misery

I will get justice for what he did to me
though it won't bring back my loved ones he took from me
it'll be satisfying and bring me peace of mind
once I've taken him down for good
so he won't terrorize anyone ever again

I won't sit in the dark
when the shadow man appears again
I will jump into the flames
of his cat and mouse games
I'll put up a stronger fight
so he won't bring me more pain and misery

Sadly, he gets to live
every day he alternates the winds of fate
does he have a conscious or feel remorse
when he brings pain and sorrow to the living

When we have another showdown
I won't let the darkness and sorrow
overpower and drown me as it did before
I will be one second quicker
to pull the trigger, and end his reign of terror for good.

In the Silence
(2020)

I walk on the grassy field
where my favorite amusement park once stood
I sit down on a rock, close my eyes, take a deep breath
and in the silence, I envision that it's 1995
my brother and I are racing off into the crowd
to get a great spot in line at one of the rides
thousands of other guests are
walking, talking, waiting in lines
I hear their conversations and excitement in their voices

We get in line for the elephant carousel ride
behind us is the swimming pool
I smell the chlorine and suntan lotion
I hear the splashing of water
maybe I'll go swimming later
since it's the beginning of the day
as we get on the ride, the lap bar falls against my knees
then we go around and around

Next, we get in line for The Serpent
the screams of the riders are loud
as the rollercoaster goes up the hill
the wheels of the car grind against the metal
my heart races in preparation
of the three-minute ride
even though I've ridden it a dozen times

Afterward, we walk to the cowboy town and the arcade
feeding the coin slots of the games
trying to amass as many tickets as we can
to win the prizes, they have on hand
as we're about to play
a buzzer goes off
alerting everyone someone hit the jackpot
and the tickets are coming out making one kid thrilled

The smell of taffy, hotdogs, and ice cream
fill the air as walk by the food booths
I look up at the people riding the sky-lift
someone cries out as their shoe drops into the lake
the sky-lift scares me since it breaks down
being stuck forty feet in the air is something I try to avoid
now it's time to go down the big yellow slide in brown sacks

The sun is now setting
we're packing up to go home
I'm sunburnt but full of excitement
it was another perfect summer day
I open my eyes
I'm back in the grassy field
I sit and wonder where all the sounds
of the rides, games, conversations, the laughs
and screams from all the years of the guests went to
did they disappear forever
or did they get trapped in the ground

Where there was once joy and excitement
is now an open field of green grass
filled with an eerie silence.

Poet's Lament

Crumpled up papers scattered on my floor
just like the ideas in my head
I have a lot of poems to write
but can't seem to get the words to flow
they're tangled up in my mind
I can't seem to form the right stanzas
and my head hurts from forcing myself to write

There are notebooks stacked high on my desk
filled with half-written poems from last year
it's anybody's guess when I'll get to them
or if I'll ever find the right words to finish them
I feel like I'm drifting aimlessly
searching for the perfect lines to create the ideal poem

I also have unopened packs of filler paper
and sharpened pencils that I could use
Lord, I'd like to phone a friend
have them help me get organized
so I can focus on my thoughts
and get the words to flow again
but in the end, it's still up to me to do the writing

When I finally sit down to write
my phone rings, my dog wants to go outside
I get new notifications on my apps
I'm getting hungry
so I enjoy a nice big bowl of ice cream and watch tv
now it's after midnight

I'm restless, I can't fall asleep
until I write something down
I have the ideas and plots
of all the poems I want to write
but my hand is being stubborn
and doesn't want to hold a pencil
help me God, give me some mercy
I'm only a poet that has target fixation
I'm running straight into a wall
to crash and burn
all because there are poems that I need to write.

Time

What is time
are we slaves to the hands
that belong to a face that we can't see
why do we allow jobs and schools
tell us when we can come and go
why can't we make our own schedules

How would we react if clocks and calendars disappeared
would we continue with our lives
as if nothing has changed
or would we believe
we now have an eternity to achieve the things we want to do
without giving it a second thought

Would we sleep during the day
then explore the world at night
to see it in a new light
would we still fear the dark
if everyone was awake with us
or would we eventually go mad
not knowing what day and time it was

Time is a funny thing
we believe we must make daily plans
only because we're taught
that time management is essential
and we only have twenty-four hours in a day
but what if we get rid of that notion
we could live without interruption
even when it's night.

Dash

What will your dash be
between your birth and death
are you leaving behind a legacy
that people will remember
or will they forget it down the line
when you're no longer mentioned by family or friends
strangers will walk by your tombstone
only your name, your year of birth and death
will be on your grave
your dash will be a mystery

I enjoy looking at tombstones from the 1800s
wondering what kind of life they lived
what did they like most about their life
did they travel from another country
were they a witness to historic events
do they still have relatives that are still alive
who can tell stories since their dash can't speak for them

It makes me wonder how people will view my dash
two-hundred years after I die
am I living a great legacy so that my story can still be told
for generations to come
or will I be forgotten through the sands of time

So when you come upon a graveyard
pay your respects for those who passed on
for they were once alive like you and me
and have a story to tell.

Heaven

God, I know the heart of man will never fully understand
what you have in store
and what waits for us behind the golden gates
after we take our last breath in this world
though I hear the streets are made of gold
there'll be no more pain, illness, or tears
there'll be all day feasting and praising
life will be perfect in every way
but I must ask

Will heaven be like our world
hanging out with family and friends
eating and drinking while watching my favorite shows
can I have my baseball memorabilia and toys
play video games and go fishing in streams
watch a Cubs game with my grandpa
or be in the kitchen with my grandma Smith
with soft-baked cookies, Kool-Aid, and play-dough

As I get older, I'm finding it hard to adjust
time is flying by so fast
each moment passes by in a blink of an eye
in my free time, I wonder
what heaven will be like when I take my last breath
and what it will be like to live forever
with all my loved ones again

Will heaven be like our world
will there be birthdays to celebrate
will there be holidays and presents
will there be pasta, steak, chicken, pizza
fruit salad, cookies, cake, and ice cream
because I admit I'm afraid to let go
I'm having too much fun in this world
and I have a lot of living to do before I die
even though I know heaven is the greatest place to be
I'm not ready to enter the golden gates.

Alternate Twilight

The more I keep track of time
the faster the hands go around and around
2011 to 2017 is all a blur
all my memories are lump together
I hurt my brain trying to untangle it all
funny though, I can recall most of my childhood
and it only seems like yesterday

Though things change
the world keeps spinning, life goes on
but I dream and wonder
what if I did things differently
would I be the person I am today
what if my mom and aunt Sue didn't pass away
I wouldn't have the poems I wrote for them
my first two books would be incomplete
but they died way too young
and should still be here

Every choice we make in the present
affects us down the line
if only we could get a sneak peek
into an alternate twilight
get to see how life could be
getting to see every outcome before making a choice
I would weigh each option before choosing the road
I'd head down

Would I redo it all if given a chance
return to my past when everything was right in this world
or would I stay in the present
either way, I should take more chances
step outside my comfort zone
dare to dream and soar with the eagles
or will I continue to build up more walls
so I'll never feel hurt and pain again
could I enjoy the unlimited sunshine
or do I need the rain

Though things change
the world keeps spinning, life goes on
I still feel you around me
guiding me along to my destiny
I'm in no hurry so I take it slow
I examine each option
pounce when the timing is right
there's a vast difference between day and night
I feel most alive when the stars are shining bright

It would be a hard choice
if I could alter the hands of time
would I stay in the present
or would I want to produce a butterfly effect
that'll cause ripples and mess with everyone's timeline.

Chapter Eight

The devil is in the Details

The devil is in the Details

The devil is in the details
if you look close enough
there's always more than meets the eye
some cards are at play
some are hiding away for another day
aces in the hole
held by those who want to alter and control our lives

You can counter attack
with your very own aces
if you have no tell
and don't wager all your chips in the first round
you can change the way the game is played
by keeping a straight face

If I don't have a gun to my back
I consider myself free to decide my destiny
to make my own choices
I'll listen to those in need
lend a helping hand
but I'm wary of those who reach out
when I can't see their intentions clearly

The devil is in the details
if you look close enough
there's always more than meets the eye
some cards are at play
some are hiding away for another day
aces in the hole
held by those who want to alter and control our lives.

The devil also Dances

I'd love to have millions of dollars
unlimited gas to travel the world
I'd love to have the power to control time
so I can relive the good times over and over
but I better keep my thoughts low
or the devil will show up at my door

The devil also dances
he's a keen observer with his ears perked up
listening to anyone who wishes for greed, power, money
desires of the heart that aren't pure
he'll appear to you as an angel of light
promise you the world that you desire
if you sign on the dotted line
oh, the devil also dances
he'll take you for a ride
and will go a few rounds on the dance floor
to gain control of your soul

I want the perfect girl
who'll greet me when I get home
have dinner every night by candlelight
make love all night
go on long weekend trips
makes it hard for us to leave for work
give her all the jewels in the world
to show her how much I adore her
I'll worship the ground she walks on
but I know a love like that won't last

The devil also dances
he's a keen observer with his ears perked up
listening to anyone who wishes for
love, adoration, unbridled passion
desires of the heart that always aren't pure
he'll appear to you as an angel of light
promise you the love that you desire
if you sign on the dotted line
oh, the devil also dances
he'll take you for a ride
and will go a few rounds on the dance floor
to gain control of your soul

Once his claws are in your veins
it's hard to make your escape
he's given you everything you ever desired
now it's time to pay up
time for him to collect his due
though you're not ready to go
he's ready to take your soul
to the underworld.

The devil's Bar

If the devil owned a bar
your bartender would be your vindictive ex
giving you guilt about leaving them
and water down the drinks
the peanuts and pretzels would be stale
there'll be a guy named Dale
who'll talk your ear off

The jukebox would only play upbeat songs
so you can't drown your sorrows
the live band will include guitars that aren't in tune
the drummer won't keep the beat
while the fiddles and violins will squeal
and hurt your ears

There'll be no light at the end of the bottle
there'll be two demons on your shoulders
praising you on your life choices
the same two voices
who sold you half-truths and lies
you can't secure salvation
at the devil's bar

The neon lights would be flames
there'll be no happy hour
the menu will consist of bland chicken wings
Cricket will be the only sport on tv
no one will care about your pleas
you won't be able to leave
there's only hisses and growls
at the devil's bar.

The devil's Rain

I've seen rain falling on sunny days
I've heard thunder echo across the land
I've seen the dark clouds sneak up on the sun
made noon look like the dead of night
I've heard the wind whisper bad things
I've seen trees turned into twigs
and it's the devil's rain that turns man away from God

I've seen it flood the mighty Mississippi
batter the coast from Florida to Maine
I've seen it sweep away my friends
all we can do is pray
because when the demons come to play
they bring the devil's rain

I've seen it tempt men, turn their eyes red
I've seen hearts bled of their purity
I've seen the holiest of men brought down to their knees
begging for their souls to be saved
as they're being buried under flowers
being watered by the devil's rain

I've seen rain falling on sunny days
I've heard thunder echo across the land
I've seen the dark clouds sneak up on the sun
made noon look like the dead of night
I've heard the wind whisper bad things
I've seen trees turned into twigs
and it's the devil's rain that turns man away from God.

Joe Tallarigo

Devil's Land

Evil spirits scour the woods
preying on lost souls
outside the farmhouse demons dwell
at the bottom of the well
in the basement where no one goes
there's a portal to hell
you can say the devil possesses the land
brought forth by man's hand

The darkness and heaviness
will make any Christian violently ill
a crooked enter at your own risk sign
hangs on the rusted gate
a warning for those brave enough seeking a thrill
though many come out changed
when they exit the devil's land
they refuse to talk about what they observed
or felt crawling on their skin

Priest after priest, even a bishop tried to cleanse the land
but it only made the entities angrier and stronger
they ripped the crosses out of the priests and bishop hands
bible pages flipped violently as caught in a fierce gust
demons hissed and growled
doors opened and slammed shut
it now seems the only way for this evil
to be banished from this land
is to have Michael the Arch Angel takes charge
and lead the angels into battle

Heaven shook as lightning lit up the noon sky
God was angry with the evil living upon his land
a trumpet sounded as Michael gripped his sword
told the demons and devil this is your last chance
to leave on your own
they laughed and said give it your best try
we've been here hundreds of years
many tried to evict us off the devil's land
and as you can see all have failed

Michael didn't flinch as he lifted his sword
as more trumpets blared
the angels came charging forth
fire and brimstone rained down from heaven
Michael battled the devil
their swords collided, both wanting to win
the devil said to Michael
"why don't you unite with me and become free
I'll give you hundreds of acres to reign over,"

Micheal just scoffed at the Devil
as he stepped back and stuck the ground
the ground shook and opened up
the demons and devil fell into the pits of hell
the angels chained them in the fire and darkness
as Michael closed the portal
the darkness and heaviness
finally lifted off the devil's land
before long crops and grass grew
a family moved in
taking over the devil's land.

More books from Joe Tallarigo

Forever in my heart-Poems of my youth

Life goes On

Country outlaws and dark Poetry

Keep the Music Playing

www.ingramcontent.com/pod-product-compliance
Lightning Source LLC
LaVergne TN
LVHW040115080426
835507LV00039B/375